SOMETHING Else TO
SMILE
ABOUT

Other Books by Zig Ziglar

Confessions of a Grieving Christian
Over the Top—Revised and Updated
Something to Smile About

SOMETHING Else TO
SMILE
ABOUT

~

*More Encouragement
and Inspiration for Life's
Ups and Downs*

~

Zig Ziglar

OLIVER
NELSON

THOMAS NELSON PUBLISHERS
Nashville

Published in Nashville, Tennessee, by Thomas Nelson, Inc.

Unless otherwise noted, the Bible version used in this publication is THE NEW KING JAMES VERSION. Copyright © 1979, 1980, 1982, Thomas Nelson, Inc., Publishers.

Scripture quotations noted KJV are from the KING JAMES VERSION.

Library of Congress Cataloging-in-Publication Data

Ziglar, Zig.
    Something else to smile about : more encouragement and inspiration for life's ups and downs / Zig Ziglar.
        p.   c.m.
    ISBN 0-7852-6912-6
    1. Conduct of life.   2. Success.   I. Title.
BJ1581.2.Z535   1999
158—dc21   99-13333
                                                                CIP

Printed in the United States of America.

4 5 6 BVG 04 03 02

~

To Laurie Magers, my loyal executive assistant of more than twenty-one years.

She is the personification of loyalty, efficiency, effectiveness, hard work, and a spirit of positive, cheerful helpfulness.

Her faith and commitment and the words of wisdom she has shared with me over the years have helped me shine more brightly than I possibly could have without her.

Contents

~

CONTENTS

Introduction

≈

The title of this book could just as well have been *Something Else to Think About* or *Food for Thought* or even *A Guideline for Daily Living*. This inspiring little volume will truly give you something to smile about and something to think about as well as pertinent information to increase your enjoyment of life and your effectiveness as a person.

In this fun book you will find a wide range of inspirational readings designed either to give you a lift for the moment or to increase your hope for the future. For maximum benefit, I encourage you to read each of the short messages and then ask yourself these questions:

- How can I apply this to my personal, family, and business lives?

- Can I use what I've just read to enhance my financial position?
- Do I know people who would relate specifically to this story and who would benefit if I shared it with them?

Taking a few moments to answer these questions will help you put what you have learned into action and will motivate you to consider the people you share your life with and how you might be of service to them.

The best use undoubtedly comes as you share the information with friends and associates. Roundtable discussions at home or in staff meetings at the office on a specific topic might generate some unexpected bonuses in the form of ideas.

I encourage you to keep *Something Else to Smile About* handy because, from time to time, all of us have little interludes that take us down and not up. Keep your pen and paper handy as you read, and when a thought or an idea is triggered, immediately write it down. By the time you finish the book you'll be pleasantly surprised at the number of ideas these simple little messages have generated, all of which will increase your enjoyment of living and, quite possibly, your standard of living. When you are happier and more fulfilled, you will undoubtedly have found *Something Else to Smile About.*

SOMETHING Else TO

SMILE

ABOUT

You Are What You
Think About

If you learn only methods, you'll be tied to your methods, but if you learn principles you can devise your own methods.

—RALPH WALDO EMERSON

The above heading has been kicked around for a long time. One enthusiastic young man said he knew it wasn't true because if he was what he thought about, he'd be a girl. There is a great deal of truth in that statement, and it leaves us with the question: What influences our thinking?

I believe that what goes into our minds and the people we associate with influence our thinking. Our thinking influences our actions. Our actions influence our performance. Our performance plays a major role in how successful and happy our future will be.

Have you ever gone to a movie and laughed? Have you ever gone to a movie and cried? Do you really think they put something in the seats that caused you to either laugh or cry? Naturally, you know better. It was what you saw on the screen that made you react with laughter or tears.

The question is, If input can make us laugh or cry, can it also make us helpful or hurtful to others? Two examples say yes. In one episode of *Happy Days*, Henry Winkler as "The Fonz" took out a library card. The American Library Association reported that after that show aired, more than 100,000 teenagers across America took out library cards. On a recent *Oprah* show, The Gap apparel chain had a fashion show featuring their new line of jeans. This was not a paid commercial; it was simply a showing of new fashions. Within seventy-two hours The Gap sold out of those jeans nationwide. In the words of Senator Paul Simon, "If thirty seconds sells soap and thirty seconds sells a car, then twenty-five minutes of glamorized violence sells violence."

Message: Be careful about what you feed your mind because it's going to affect your actions—which will affect your future.

~

As Groucho Marx once said, "Who are you going to believe, me or your own eyes?"

Fixing Problems

You don't "forget" negative thinking—you force it out with positive input.

Question: Can you remember a day when you did not have some "problem," irritation, disappointment, defeat, or setback of some kind? It might be having to make an unexpected stop at the service station because your mate drove your car and neglected to refill it. Or maybe your boss gave you incomplete information on an important project and now you have to start all over.

The big issue is not the problems; they're part of life. The issue is how to handle the problems. Do you let a simple problem dictate how you should behave the rest of the day, even the way you deal with other people? Sometimes it's hard to do, but ask yourself the question, *What real difference does this make in my life tonight, or even in the morning?* In most cases you'll realize that it really doesn't matter. With that in mind, you'll be able to forget the problem of the moment and move on.

Conclusion: You can take control of your own thoughts, actions, and emotions, which means you can take control of your life. The best way to deal with problems is to reorder your thinking and see them as opportunities to grow or mature. It also helps to remember that if there were no problems in your job, chances are good you would not be needed. Chances are also good that the greater the difficulties, the greater the need for you to be there to handle them. That's the reason you're on the payroll.

~

It was not so long ago that people thought semiconductors were part-time orchestra leaders and microchips were very, very small snack foods. (GERALDINE FERRARO)

Make Way for
"Uncle No-Name"

You achieve customer satisfaction when you sell merchandise that doesn't come back to a customer who does.

—STANLEY MARCUS

His name was Wally Amos and he built a $100 million business selling his "Famous Amos Cookies." Through a series of unfortunate circumstances, he lost his business. He went from fame and fortune to a debt level of $1 million. Even worse, he lost the right to use the name he made famous. He did not, however, lose the things that made him successful in the first place. He maintained his sense of humor and his outgoing, optimistic, confident nature. As might be expected, he bounced back big-time.

He started a new venture under the name of "Wally Amos Presents Chip'n Cookie." *People* magazine did a story and Fitz & Floyd made a Chip'n Cookie jar. J.C. Penney marketed Chip'n Cookie dolls. Everyone was delighted at Mr. Amos's comeback. Everybody but the new owners of "Famous Amos." A lawsuit resulted and once again he was put out of business. Wally says he got famous and rich and paid a price for it. Today he is on tour promoting his new book, *Man with No Name,* which is being enthusiastically received. He is also back in the cookie business. His new company, "Uncle No-Name," got under way in November. Obviously, he is a good example of a man being knocked down but not out. He is fighting back with the same zest and zeal he demonstrated the first time around. I predict he will do well.

Wally Amos is the classic example of a man who gets up again and again. The old saying that a person who won't be beat can't be beat is certainly true of "Uncle No-Name."

~

They tell us to keep in touch with our bodies. Today I said to my body, "How'd you like to go to the gym and do three hours of heavy aerobics?" My body responded, "Do it and you'd die."

Change Can Be
Good for You

We get comfort from those who agree with us and growth from those who don't.

In today's world of societal and corporate change, job security is a thing of the past. While we must face the fact that change is inevitable, we should also realize that many changes are positive and benefit both individuals and businesses.

Some things you can change and some you can't. You cannot change when you were born, where you were born, how you were born, or to whom you were born. It's a fact that if you were born white you will stay white and if you were born black you will remain black. It's a fact that you cannot change a single event that has already happened. You can't change one whisper of yesterday. Tomorrow, however, is an entirely different matter. If you're willing to change your thinking today, you can change your life and your living to make your tomorrows better and brighter.

Example: As a student at Yazoo City High School in Mississippi, table tennis was one of my favorite sports. Frankly, I could beat most of my buddies at that particular sport. Then a new kid came to town and he beat me regularly. I was using the old three-finger grip; he was using the new "handshake" grip. I felt that I was playing as well as I could with the grip I was using so I changed to the "handshake" grip. Initial results were disastrous. My buddies beat me like a drum. But after a couple of weeks I started winning and eventually was able to beat the "new kid in town." I'm convinced there was no way I could have done that without changing my grip, though I actually got worse at first.

Message: Analyze your situation. Have you gone as far as you can go and are you doing as well as you can with present procedures? If so, don't be afraid to take two steps back if it will enable you to move three steps forward.

~

Boss, as he fires an employee: "Look on the bright side. You always said you wanted to be an entrepreneur."

Let Your Reach
Exceed Your Grasp

Motivation is needed to change the costume of the dream to the work clothes of reality based on the goals generated by the dream.

In one of our major universities a professor of economics gave a test to his class. The test had several sections of questions, each of which contained three categories of questions. He instructed the students to choose one question from each section on the test. The first category in each section was the hardest and was worth 50 points. The second category in each section was not quite as hard and worth 40 points. The third category in each section was the easiest and worth only 30 points.

When the students had taken the test and all the papers had been turned in, the students who had chosen the hardest questions, or the 50-point questions, were given A's. The students who had chosen the 40-point questions were given B's, and the students choosing the 30-point questions, or the easiest questions, were given C's. Whether or not their answers were correct was not considered. Understandably, the students were confused and asked the professor how he had graded the exam. The professor leaned back and with a smile explained, "I wasn't testing your knowledge. I was testing your aim."

I believe it was Browning who said, "Your reach should exceed your grasp, or what's a heaven for?" Langston Hughes wrote, "Hold fast to dreams, for if dreams die then life is like a broken-winged bird that cannot fly." Yes, we need those dreams or, if you prefer, a vision. Solomon, the wisest man who ever lived, said, "Where there is no vision, the people perish" (Prov. 29:18 KJV). Helen Keller was asked the question, "What would be worse than being blind?" She responded that it would be infinitely worse to have 20/20 eyesight and no vision than to be blind but have that vision.

In the declining years of his life, Albert Schweitzer was asked, "How goes it with you, Dr. Schweitzer?" The aging medical missionary responded, "My eyesight grows dim, but my vision is clearer than ever."

∽

If you ever think you're too small to be effective, you've never been in bed with a mosquito. (ANITA RODDICK)

Getting Out of the Box

It is not the brains that matter most, but that which guides them—the character, the heart, generous qualities, progressive ideas.

—FYODOR DOSTOYEVSKY

Many people set low ceilings on their expectations and capabilities. In the process, they place themselves in a "box." Alexander Whortley took that a step farther and literally lived in a box. It was a mini-trailer, three feet wide, four feet long, and five feet high. He lived there until he died at the age of eighty. His box was made of wood, had a metal roof, and it housed him and all his meager belongings. Regardless of where he worked, Whortley chose to spend his life in that cramped space, even though larger, more comfortable quarters were always available.

Few of us live in a "box." However, too many of us have a tendency to "box" ourselves in and continue to do things one way because we've "always done it this way." In many cases, time and experience have proved that "this way" is the best way. However, I challenge you to periodically take a long walk or quietly sit and think about the way you do things. Ask yourself if there might not be a better way. Could your procedures be simplified? Are they necessary at all? Could they be done more cheaply or efficiently? Could your product be longer? Shorter? A different shape? Another fabric? Another color? Sometimes you can come up with simple ideas that make a big difference. Incidentally, one advantage of a way of life that includes continual personal growth and education is that the broader and deeper your knowledge base, the more creative your problem-solving approach to life.

Simple example: For years men's coats had an inside pocket only on the right where pens and other items were kept. One day somebody had a thought: *Since most men are right-handed, why not put a pocket on the inside left so that they could reach in, extract the pen with their right hand, and begin writing?* Not monumental, but it saves a second or two and it's sold lots of suits.

~

In an election year we should not be surprised the air is filled with speeches and vice versa. (Political speechwriter JOSEPH NOLAN)

Never Follow a Bad Shot
with a Bad Decision

Great fear will always lose out to great faith.

As an avid golfer I'm often puzzled by the actions of the typical high-handicap golfer. He steps up to the tee box and with driver in hand takes his stance, thinks the shot through, and hits the ball about 210 yards out and about 40 yards to the right, where it lands in the midst of some trees. He walks or rides to the ball, looks at the six-foot opening, and determines that all he's got to do to reach the green is hit the ball 175 yards through that opening, send it over the lake, and fade it over the bunker to land on the green.

Let me remind you of the scenario: He just missed a fairway roughly sixty yards wide with the ball teed up and in perfect position. For his second shot he believes he can go through a six-foot opening and make the ball act as it does when one of the top touring pros on the PGA hits it. With the confidence that generally goes with ignorance, he steps up, fires away, and hits the ball into the lake. In anger and disgust, he then hits the ball over the green into a sand bunker. Two strokes later he is on the green where he two-putts for a disastrous quadruple-bogey-8. He followed a bad shot with a bad decision and it cost him.

Too often all of us hit a "bad shot" (e.g., make a mistake, handle the truth loosely). Then we compound that "bad shot" by denying it, defending it, lying about it, or rationalizing it instead of quietly thinking it through, acknowledging the mistake, and working through it in a logical, forthright manner.

～

As the stock market joke goes about your investments, the broker makes money, the broker's firm makes money, and two out of three's not bad.

Gossip Is Enormously Destructive

Warm hearts seldom produce hot heads.

We frequently hear little jokes about gossip, like the two people who were talking and one said, "I can't tell you any more. I've already told you more than I heard." In that line is much of the tragedy about gossip, which can, and often has, destroyed a person's reputation. Gossip always damages relationships, specifically with the person you are gossiping about. For example, once you have said something unkind about a person, you will feel uncomfortable around them and your relationship with them will suffer.

Dr. Adrian Rogers wisely points out that before we disseminate information that might be considered gossip, we must carefully ponder three questions: Number one, Is it the truth? If it fails the first test, then it is not repeatable. Number two, even if it is the truth, Do you really need to share it? Will it help anyone? Will it hurt anyone? Would it be better left unsaid? If there are no benefits to anyone, then what possible purpose could repeating it serve? Number three, Is it kind? In our world so full of cynicism and skepticism, will repeating this story be kind? Would it be better left unsaid? Would you really be better off repeating this information? When you analyze it this way, your chances of being a gossiper are dramatically reduced.

When you consider the benefits of stopping gossip in its tracks, you'll discover they're substantial. First, you do not damage yourself, which means that your reputation and esteem are untarnished. That's good. Second, you won't harm someone else's reputation. This means that your circle of friends will be larger. Since most of us do not have any friends we would like to lose, that's good!

~

A class reunion has been defined as an occasion when you meet people who used to be the same age as you.

Where There's a Will There's a Way

Mountaintops inspire leaders but valleys mature them.

—J. PHILIP EVERSON

Dr. William "Bill" Ross was truly one of a kind and was known for his sense of humor and his zest for life. He had an exuberance for living, a love for medicine, and a concern for his patients that is seldom equaled. Dr. Ron Anderson of Parkland Memorial Hospital said, "When one of his patients died or got sick, it hurt him, but he also celebrated with them when they recovered."

He was elected president of the Texas Medical Association in 1981 and received numerous honors and recognition. He received his undergraduate degree from Stephen F. Austin University and worked his way through the University of Texas Southwestern Medical School at Dallas by selling watermelons. He interned at Parkland Memorial Hospital and later moved to San Benito, Texas. When he arrived, Dr. Ross was told there was not room for another doctor, but he chose not to take their advice to move on. He built his practice in a simple but effective way. On house calls he would deliberately go to the incorrect house to the right side of the correct address and introduce himself. They told him where the correct house was but he repeated the process at the house to the left of the correct one. Three months later he had a thriving practice.

Dr. Ross helped build the University of Texas Southwestern Medical School at Dallas into a premier training ground for family practitioners. However, he is well remembered for his first day on the job. He arrived at the school wearing overalls and driving a pickup truck. Later he said it was like "two culture shocks—theirs and mine." However, behind that "country" demeanor were a brilliant mind and a commitment to medicine, wrapped up in a love for his fellowman, which made him a standout in the medical world. Come to think about it, the qualities I just identified will be useful to anyone, whatever their profession.

~

Even though people know how they're supposed to behave, sometimes they forget. That's why they hold church every Sunday.

Those "Good Ol' Days"

Today is the tomorrow you were optimistic about yesterday. Question: What are you doing today to make tomorrow as rewarding as you hoped today would be?

A popular joke goes like this: A former athlete (teacher, preacher, coach, etc.) laughingly says, "The older I get, the better I was!" There's more truth than fiction in that statement and, in a way, that's good. It certainly indicates the person is looking back and thinking of the good things instead of the negatives of life. That kind of attitude will ensure not only a longer life, but a happier and healthier one to boot!

Realistically speaking, many of our memories about the "good ol' days" do not deal with facts. In those "good ol' days" of 150 years ago, life expectancy was approximately forty years. Today it is nearly seventy. When I was a youngster, polio was the scourge of the day. Every parent feared polio when they sent their son or daughter outside to play during the hot summer months. Today, thanks to the vaccine, polio is rare.

Currently, more than 80 percent of millionaires in

America are first-generation millionaires. Women are earning respect in the worlds of business, medicine, science, education, athletics, and other fields that were denied them just a few years ago. In today's America there are more minorities with college educations and in the upper echelon of business than ever before. This is not to suggest that everything is equal, but it does say that we're making progress.

Success has been defined as a journey, not a destination—but we must be headed in the right direction. Despite our problems with crime, welfare, drugs, and violence, there are few people who would return to the "good ol' days." Yes, things are better today than they ever have been. We have problems as a nation, but we are actively seeking solutions. For that reason, "these are the good ol' days." I encourage you to enjoy today and look to the future with optimism and hope.

~

Little League baseball in our town is going a little too far. Now they're trying to trade my kid to Cleveland.

Where Will the Records Stop?

Success is not measured by what a man accomplishes, but by the opposition he has encountered and the courage with which he has maintained the struggle against overwhelming odds.

—ORRISON SWETT MARDEN

In 1954 Roger Bannister ran a sub-four-minute mile and it ignited the athletic world. In 1994, Eamonn Coghlan of Ireland, at age forty-one, ran a sub-four-minute mile. Incredibly enough, Kip Keino of Ethiopia, at age fifty-five, ran a 4.06-minute mile.

By 1954 more than fifty medical journals had published articles saying that the four-minute mile was not humanly possible. Doctors were warning athletes of the dire consequences to anyone who broke that "unbreakable" barrier. In the meantime, coaches all over the world, with stopwatches in hand, were encouraging their charges to do their best—but to forget about breaking the "impossible" four-minute barrier.

Roger Bannister broke the barrier and changed that thinking by his performance. He refused to believe what others were saying because he didn't want to limit his own potential. His breakthrough proved that the barrier was psychological, not physiological. In the August 1994 *Runner's World* magazine, Jerry Lynch, Ph.D., said that when you believe and think *I can,* you activate your motivation, commitment, confidence, concentration, and excitement, all of which relate directly to achievement. On the other hand, "Whether you think you can or think you can't, you're right in both cases."

Dr. Lynch says that the path to personal excellence is cluttered with obstacles. It is my personal conviction that you can't develop your full potential without encountering serious obstacles along the way. Dr. Lynch also says that you can't stretch your limits without encountering some rough moments. You need to understand that failure and losses are acceptable learning experiences that can help improve your performance. This is true in every part of life, whether it involves athletics, academic achievement, business, or sales success. It's true that airplanes and kites rise fastest when they fly into the wind. Individuals grow stronger physically, mentally, and spiritually when they are "tested" with resistance or opposition.

～

As legendary Green Bay Packer coach Vince Lombardi used to say about his team, "Careful. You're playing with live ammunition!"

Failure Is Critical to Success

With dreams there's no need to go to dreamland via drugs and alcohol.

You've got to learn to lose in order to win" sounds like strange advice, but the man who says it has earned over $300 million. Even in today's economy, that's a considerable sum of money. Here's the story.

In 1958 Frank and Dan Carney started a pizza parlor across from their family's grocery store. Their goal was to pay for their college educations. Nineteen years later, Frank Carney sold the 3,100-outlet chain called "Pizza Hut" for $300 million.

Carney's advice to those starting out in business sounds strange, but he explains the concept this way: "I've been involved in about fifty different business ventures and about fifteen of them were successful. That means I have about a thirty percent success average." The major point Frank makes is this: You need to be "at bat" if you ever expect to get a hit, and it's even more important to step back up to the plate after you strike out.

Carney says Pizza Hut was successful because he learned from his mistakes. For example, when an

Oklahoma City expansion effort failed, he realized the importance of location and decor. He learned from his mistake so that the future would be brighter. When sales declined in New York, he came up with the innovative idea of introducing thick crust, with substantial success. When regional pizza houses began to take part of the market share, Frank responded by introducing "Chicago-style pizza," and again success came his way. Factually, Carney failed many times but in each case he made those failures work for him.

Failure is an experience common to all of us. Question: Will you let those failures work for you or against you? If you do as Frank Carney did, you will use your failures as learning experiences.

～

Advice from an investment guru: "Send me ten dollars and I'll tell you how I became rich." So you send him ten dollars and he sends back a note saying, "Thanks. I got rich because of people like you."

Overcoming Fear

Fear is the dark room where negatives are developed.

Fear has been correctly identified with the acrostic **False Evidence Appearing Real**. The truth is that if we think something is to be feared, that perception becomes the cruelest form of reality.

A second-grade boy was overheard saying, "It's easy to be brave when you're not scared." By the same token, it's easy to talk about how to overcome fear when you have little to be afraid of. Fear is certainly real for most people and all of us face a fear of something—maybe it's poverty, divorce, rejection, death, failure, speaking in public, or being laughed at.

How do we overcome fear? First we must learn to examine our fears. Giving a speech is the number one fear in our country, according to *Reader's Digest*. (It's also a tremendous confidence-builder.) If that's your fear, ask yourself a few questions: *Why am I afraid to make a speech? Is it because I'm afraid of being rejected? If so, do I think I'll be rejected? Do I believe what I'm about to say? Is my speech worth giving? Am I proud of the comments I'm about to make? As you* ask yourself these questions, the fear will begin to subside. It subsides because you have explored your subconscious mind with your questions and flushed out some of your fears.

My research indicates that only three people have died while making a speech. Since twelve billion people have lived and only three of them died making a speech, I'd say it's a fairly safe thing to do. If you're a little nervous, consider this: You could lead a mule into a crowded room and he would be so calm that he would almost go to sleep standing up. A thoroughbred in the same situation would be as nervous as a cat. If you're a little nervous, just be grateful you're a thoroughbred—not a mule. So face those inner feelings, stand up, and speak with confidence.

∽

A frog telephones a psychic hot line and is told, "You're going to meet a beautiful young girl who will want to know everything about you." "Great!" says the frog. "Will I meet her at a party?" "No," said the psychic, "next year in biology class."

This Way to Greatness

The future never just happened—it was created.

—WILL DURANT

My friend and fellow speaker, Joe Sabah, says that you don't have to be great to start, but you have to start to be great. This is a profound observation and applies regardless of your field of endeavor. It brings to mind the story of one skinny, sickly young man who truly was the "ninety-seven-pound weakling" when he was in high school. He wore thick glasses, arch supports, and a shoulder brace. His self-image was so poor and his concern about his appearance so great that he dropped out of school. His future did not look good.

Then one day he attended a health lecture. He was inspired by what he heard and became convinced that there was something he could do about his poor physical condition. He wanted his future to be better than his past, so he started to exercise for hours every day. He also dramatically changed his eating habits. As a cumulative result of these actions, he slowly changed his appearance, his self-image, and his future.

In 1936 he opened one of the first health studios in

America because he wanted to share with others the benefits he was enjoying. He went door-to-door in Oakland, California, promoting his new exercise business. After nearly six decades he's still promoting exercise. His reputation is international and many think of him as "Mr. Exercise." He's become a financial success, but more important, he's become a success in life itself. Today he can outperform men who are fifty years his junior. His feats of strength and endurance astonish us all.

By now you've probably guessed that I'm talking about Jack LaLanne. Jack would be the first to tell you that his change of direction wasn't easy. A major change of direction won't be easy for you, either, but with Jack LaLanne as a role model, you can begin the process. Follow his example and your future will be different from and better than your past. The choice is yours.

≈

If you have a great ambition, take as big a step as possible in the direction of fulfilling it, but if the step is only a tiny one, don't worry if it is the largest one now possible. (MILDRED MCAFEE)

Identify—Then Solve—The Problem

Watch out for phony or easy solutions to complex problems. When you spot a quack, duck.

Fortunately, problems are an everyday part of our lives. Consider this: If there were no problems, most of us would be unemployed. Realistically, the more problems we have and the larger they are, the greater our value to our employer.

Of course, some problems are small, like opening a ketchup bottle. Others are monumental, like a seriously ill or injured child or mate, which presents ongoing, daily complications. Successful living comes when we learn to handle those business and personal problems with as little fanfare as possible. The successful business executive can handle challenges and solve problems at a remarkable clip. He or she makes quick and final decisions as a result of years of experience. The homemaker with small children at home handles many "catastrophes" each hour with the same dispatch.

Many people use counterproductive methods to deal with problems: They refuse to recognize them, deny responsibility for them, pretend they will go away if they ignore them, or are just flat insensitive to them. The first step in solving a problem is to recognize that it does exist. Next, we determine whether the problem is our responsibility. If the answer is yes, we must determine how serious and/or urgent it is. When that last determination is made, we either take immediate action if the problem is simple and quickly solvable or develop a plan of action and prioritize it if the solution is more difficult and time-consuming.

Problem solving becomes a very important part of our makeup as we grow into maturity or move up the corporate ladder. I encourage you to take the time to define the problem correctly, learn the skill of quick analysis and remember, if it weren't for problems in your life, your position might not be necessary in the first place. Ironing out the wrinkles and solving the problems are what most jobs are about.

∼

Small boy to mom: "You should be proud you have a child with enough guts to bring home a report card like that. Besides, you know I didn't cheat."

Reducing Health Care Costs

Do a little more than you're paid to. Give a little more
than you have to. Try a little harder than you want to.
Aim a little higher than you think possible, and give a
lot of thanks to God for health, family, and friends.

—ART LINKLETTER

According to recent newspaper articles, there is a new and unexpected way to cut health care costs. Hospitals can save big bucks by putting chaplains on their health care teams. Surprised? Hospitals are beginning to recognize that spiritual well-being can be crucial to the healing process. The Reverend George Frank, director of pastoral care at Victory Memorial Hospital in Waukegan, Illinois, says, "I don't think you can separate the physical from the emotional and spiritual. People are whole people. You can't treat the body without there being a spiritual or emotional impact."

I know that the skeptic might not agree with this idea philosophically, but I'm not talking about philosophy; I'm talking about facts. The facts are these: From 1991 to 1993, Dr. Elizabeth McSherry studied seven hundred coronary patients admitted to the Brockton/West

Roxbury, Virginia, Center. Dr. McSherry is the deputy director of a program for Veterans Administration hospitals that works to help doctors control costs and improve quality. The group studied received some of the most costly and complicated procedures available such as bypass operations, valve replacements, and open-heart surgery. Also included in the study were veterans undergoing care for heart attacks and chronic heart disease.

One group of patients had daily visits from a chaplain. The other group of patients saw a chaplain an average of three minutes during their entire hospital stay. The study found that patients who had the most contact with the chaplains were released from the hospital an average of two days sooner than patients who did not receive regular visits. Dr. McSherry estimates that the cost of the chaplain visits was no more than $100 per patient. The savings, however, from letting a patient go home earlier amounted to as much as $4,000 a day. The group visited by chaplains also had fewer complications after surgery.

Sounds like a logical way to cut our health care costs dramatically. That approach might even be a good idea for all phases of our lives.

～

One fellow had a photographic mind. Unfortunately, he never had it developed.

Observations from a Soldier

Leadership is the ability to persuade others to do what you want them to do because they want to do it.

—DWIGHT D. EISENHOWER

It is my privilege to know General Colin Powell and to have been present during a recent question and answer session with him. I believe his remarks are worth repeating.

Someone asked, "What did you learn in the military?" General Powell said the first thing he learned was that everyone was at the same level (thanks to the uniform haircut given all recruits). Other things he learned were: stand at attention and salute, which instilled discipline and obedience; to march in step and function as a part of a team while taking individual pride as a team member; that if he did not stay in step with the others there were undesirable consequences; and that if he performed well, both he and his team were recognized.

He pointed out that basic training physically hardens recruits and makes them respect their own bodies, enabling them to perform better. He observed that the first week is generally so hard and the drill sergeant so demanding that most recruits develop something akin to hatred for the sergeant. But the hatred fades quickly. By the second week of training, the typical recruit is doing everything he can to please his drill sergeant.

That is an amazing turnabout. For many recruits, the discipline is translated to love and caring for them, which is a new experience for some. The truth is, discipline is loving—just ask any parent. Discipline is essential to every individual and crucial for teams. No unit can ever become a potent fighting force without discipline and no life can be truly successful without it.

The criteria for becoming a successful soldier or a successful private citizen are the same. If we learn to function as a team member, we will do so only after we've brought our personal life under control and learned how to "drill." When you sum it all up, it really says there's something we can do about our future.

~

Army psychiatrist to young recruit: "What is the difference between a boy and a dwarf?" "Lots of difference," replied the recruit. "Give me an example," said the psychiatrist. "The dwarf might be a girl," said the recruit.

Hope in the Future

Things turn out the best for those who make the best of the way things turn out.

Dr. John Maxwell says that if there's hope in the future there is power in the present. The reason is simple: Hope in the future has a dramatic impact on your thinking today. Your thinking today determines your performance today, and your performance today has a direct bearing on your future. Dr. Tony Campolo of Eastern College in Pennsylvania says that your past is important because it brought you to where you are, but as important as your past is, it is not nearly as important as the way you see your future. He is saying, "I understand the problems of your past. I know that you were abused as a child, raised by alcoholic parents, suffered through bankruptcy, depression, and/or alcoholism. You've gone through one or more divorces. All of these things are traumatic events that affect the way you think and the way you act." In no way is Dr. Campolo denying any of the impact of your past, because many of those events are extremely significant. However, he is saying that despite all these things, the way you see your future is even more important.

John Johnson, publisher and owner of *Ebony* magazine and one of the four hundred wealthiest men in America, says that "men and women are limited not by the place of their birth, not by the color of their skin, but by the size of their hope."

Make friends with your past so you can focus on today, which will make your tomorrows even better. If you are familiar with my material, you realize that my nature is that of an optimist—I just can't see any point in being pessimistic. I'm not talking about denial of reality; what I am talking about is facing reality, but facing it in an optimistic way.

～

It may be true that most people can't handle prosperity, but it is also true that most people don't have to.

The "Seat" of Your Attitude

Admitting a mistake is a beginning; correcting it is a step forward; following through is success.

Over the years I have spoken at several thousand functions of virtually every description. I have spoken to groups of twelve and once to a throng of sixty thousand. I have consistently noted one tendency in all audiences, especially in sales organizations and leadership/management conferences. Almost without exception the top salespeople are seated at or very close to the front, depending on their vision and the angle of the seats they have chosen.

Those people who already "know it all" or feel that they do, or those people who consider this a waste of their time or think they've "heard it all before," will invariably arrive late or at the last moment, unprepared. They are also the ones most likely to squirm in their seats, leave early, or talk to the person next to them.

I've also observed that when these same people go to an athletic or entertainment event, they want the best seat in the house. They generally arrive in plenty of time and are irritated when there are distractions from anyone else.

All of this is to say that front-row people by and large come to educational or inspirational meetings with great expectations. They come prepared to learn and take good notes. A study at Harvard University revealed that people who get the most out of meetings (a) come with the expectation of getting great ideas, (b) take good notes, and (c) talk with colleagues about what they learned and compare notes. This way they reinforce what they learned and pick up points they missed from the other person. In short, these people are winners because they plan to win, prepare to win, and expect to win. That's a good approach to life.

You can't be a smart cookie if you have a crummy attitude. (JOHN MAXWELL)

Concentrate on Your Responsibilities

We cannot become what we need to be by remaining what we are.

From time to time I have the privilege of speaking to university and professional football teams. On other occasions, I have an opportunity to speak to coaches at local high school and college levels. On one of these occasions, I heard former University of Texas coach John Mackovic make an interesting observation that I believe is applicable to any field of endeavor.

He said that when his team was on the offense, he was "interested" in the defensive alignment, but was "vitally concerned" about what his players were going to do. He observed that if he had recruited the right players, coached and trained them properly, and if he and his coaches had developed a good game plan, he was confident that his team was going to score more points than the opposition.

He then reversed the observation, assuming the opposition had the ball. He was interested in what their athletes and their game plan called for, but he was "vitally concerned" about his defensive alignment and what his players were going to do. That lesson can be applied, regardless of what we do. Be interested in what others are doing, but be vitally concerned about your own performance. If coworkers are late and slack in their performance, view that as an opportunity to make a bigger contribution and climb the corporate ladder even faster.

Remember, if you're in a leadership position, your responsibility is to choose the right people, then train and inspire them to use their ability. Peter Drucker said it well: "Leadership is lifting a person's vision to higher sights, raising a person's performance to a higher standard, building a personality beyond its normal limitations." Buy that concept and your leadership effectiveness and the performance of your people will improve substantially.

~

You can tell the romance is getting serious when the girl starts asking her mom how to thaw food.

Hugging Is the Answer

Watch your thoughts, they become words. Watch your words, they become actions. Watch your actions, they become habits. Watch your habits, they become character. Watch your character, it becomes your destiny.

—MOTTO, METROPOLITAN MILWAUKEE YMCA

Perhaps I feel this way because my wife is affectionately known as "The Happy Hugger." If it's moving she'll stop it and hug it, and if it's not moving she'll dust it off and sell it! However, there's another reason I believe hugging is the answer. According to Greg Risberg of the Northwestern University Medical School in Chicago, the physiological benefits of hugging include a reduction of blood pressure and increased oxygen in the blood. He says that we all have a "skin hunger," and we are missing out on a vital part of our health if we're not getting in on some serious hugging. He maintains that four hugs a day are the minimum required to meet that skin hunger. From my perspective, I need lots more than four. Stanley Simon of the University of Massachusetts says that "hugging does

41

more than demonstrate affection. It actually seems to keep people healthy. The skin is the body's largest sensory organ. If it's understimulated, many people actually develop an aching sensation. These are the people who will find it harder to get well and to stay well."

For the benefit of you husbands, let me tell you something about your wives. They love hugs but resent it when you ignore them all day and then give them your undivided attention when the lights go out at night. They want a hug when a hug is all you have on your mind. They don't necessarily want them to be long, and in most cases, they do not want them to be suggestive or sensual. The hug really says, "I love you, I enjoy being around you, you're important to me, I look forward to spending more time with you." There's an old saying that actions speak louder than words, and to take a few seconds a number of times during the day to get and give those nonsuggestive hugs really speaks volumes. Give it a try.

~

When you act like a skunk, someone will eventually get wind of it.

Looking for Mutually Beneficial Solutions

A winner is big enough to admit his mistakes, smart enough to profit from them, and strong enough to correct them.

—JOHN MAXWELL

Every problem has a solution, but the best solutions are always mutually beneficial. Howard Putnam, in his book *The Winds of Turbulence,* tells this story. Baylor Hospital in Dallas had a major problem. They could not get enough nurses who were willing to work weekends because they wanted to be with their families. But the leadership recognized that there were also a number of nurses, particularly those who had young children, who wanted to be with their children during the week so they could spend as much time with them as possible. In most cases, married nurses had husbands who worked a Monday-through-Friday schedule. Single mothers had an even greater need to be with their children as much as possible, so the thinking was very simple: *Can we meet the needs of* all *these nurses?*

Leadership then asked the question, How can we help these mothers get what they want? How can we help the full-time nurses get what they want? The solution, as Mr. Putnam points out, was so obvious, one wonders why it took them so long to come up with the answer. Here's what they did: Since weekend work is generally considered overtime, they decided to make Saturday and Sunday twelve-hour shifts, for a total of twenty-four hours of duty. They paid these nurses for a full forty-hour week, so those nurses were elated to be able to get that kind of duty. On the other hand, the nurses who simply did not want to work overtime or weekends were elated that they could maintain their normal schedule. This truly was a win-win situation. The weekend nurses won, the full-time nurses won, and the hospital and patients were also big winners.

That's leadership at its best. The message is clear: Examine your alternatives; explore what the problem might be and ask yourself the question, *Is the solution in the problem?* In many cases it is.

∼

My problem is that I'm always good when nobody is watching. (DENNIS THE MENACE)

They All Did Well

You have been given citizenship in a country like none other on earth, with opportunities available to you like nowhere else on earth. All we ask of you is hard work; nothing will be handed to you. Use your education and success in life to help those still trapped in cycles of poverty and violence. Above all, never lose faith in America. Its faults are yours to fix, not to curse.

—GENERAL COLIN POWELL

Today I'd like to talk about a remarkable family from inner-city New Orleans, the Lundy-Smiths. Susie Mae Lundy and her husband, Willie J. Smith, a Baptist pastor, raised nine successful children. According to *Fortune* magazine, the parents set an entrepreneurial example built around commitment, faith, and hard work. Each child grew up with assigned responsibilities. By age five the six boys were expected to hose down and sweep the driveway of the family's Exxon gas station and auto repair shop. Son Larry, owner of thirty-one Pizza Hut outlets, says they knew that what the family ate at the end of the day was contingent upon

45

what they did during the day. That kind of motivation is pretty easy to understand—and can be very effective.

Today, Michael is a Mobil Oil executive in Houston; Harold is president of Louisiana's Grambling State University; Mark and Wilton are psychiatric counselors in Houston; Nell is an elementary school teacher in Houston; Lloyd is a vice president at Goodwill Industries in Beaumont, Texas; Jackie is an emergency room nurse and Yolanda is an accountant, both in New Orleans. All of them are hardworking, productive citizens and they started early. Back in 1978 all the kids led a fund-raising drive that raised about $65,000 to build the church their father now leads. These "kids" have also presented their parents with fourteen grandchildren and three great-grandchildren.

Yes, it looks like the American Dream is still alive for those who are willing to work hard and dream that American Dream, particularly if they have parents who guide and direct them early on.

≈

This town on the coast was so dull that when the tide went out it refused to come back.

"We're Both on the Same Side"

*Remember that when you're standing on the edge of
a cliff, the best way to make progress is to back up.*

One of my favorite stories concerns a young lad who
was confronted by three bullies with violence in mind.
Quickly, the little guy drew a line on the ground,
stepped back several feet, looked the biggest bully in the
eye and said, "Now, you just step over that line."
Confidently, the big bully stepped over the line, preparing to commit mayhem on the little guy. Quickly the
little fellow grinned and said, "Now we're both on the
same side."

Physically, they were both on the same side. But
emotionally they were still some distance apart. The
smaller boy improved his chances of getting on the same
side emotionally by his touch of wit and wisdom. This
is an excellent combination to diffuse most crisis situa-
tions and represents a major step in solving whatever
problems exist.

There are several lessons parents, managers, and
educators can learn from this little vignette. First,
whether it is a parent-child, management-labor, or

teacher-student situation, both really are on the same side and the best way for either side to win is for both sides to win. Second, a sense of humor can be very helpful in removing communications barriers by revealing your human side and establishing rapport. Third, sometimes it's necessary for the big bully (the person in authority) to move to the other side of the table (across the line). This lets associates, children, or employees clearly understand that they really are on the same side and open to listening to ideas from both sides of that line. The fourth message is that it is always important and to our advantage to maintain our perspective by being open and fair-minded as we look at life from the other person's perspective.

∼

Enjoy your kids while they're young and still on your side.

She Passed the Test—Can You?

It's okay to retire from a job but you should never retire from work.

Major surgery requires not only a skilled surgeon, but a number of skilled assistants to make certain that everything happens as it should. They function as a team. No one person, regardless of how brilliant they are, could pull off a major operation alone.

Recently, in a major medical center, a new head nurse was starting her first assignment. She was in charge of all the nurses on the operating room team. She had full responsibility for performing all the duties nurses perform. When the surgery was complete, the surgeon said, "Okay, it's time to close the incision. I need the sutures." The new head nurse responded, "Doctor, you used twelve sponges; we've only removed eleven." The surgeon assured her that all of the sponges had been removed and he was ready to suture. She replied, "Doctor, you used twelve sponges; only eleven have been removed." With a bit of irritation in his voice, the doctor said, "I will accept full responsibility." At that point, the nurse's temper flew and she apparently stomped her foot and said, "Doctor, think of the patient!" When she said that, the doctor smiled, lifted his foot, and revealed the twelfth sponge. He looked at the nurse and said, "You'll do." Her integrity had been tested; she passed with flying colors.

The question is, How many of us, under identical circumstances, would have risked offending the surgeon, remembering that there was a possibility we had miscounted? But this nurse felt the patient's life and health were at stake and she, without hesitation, did the right thing. Over the long haul, that's the best way to get to the top and stay there.

~

Team-builders are the tea bags of life. They perform when the water is hot. (ROGER STAUBACH)

A Philosophy to Live By

Successful people tell others how to get on, not where to get off.

Wisdom goes back a long way and comes in the form of examples, illustrations, stories, clichés, parables, etc. One of the oldest bits of philosophy says that "for want of a nail a shoe was lost, for want of a shoe a horse was lost, for want of a horse a rider was lost, for want of a rider a leader was lost, for want of a leader a battle was lost, for want of a victory a war was lost, for want of a plan a nation was lost."

One variation of that could well be in the form of some ancient Chinese philosophies, which are frequently rich in wisdom and truth. They carry truths that apply to people and nations, regardless of the century in which we're living. One of those gems is: "If there is righteousness in the heart, there will be duty in the character. If there is duty in the character, there will be harmony in the home. If there is harmony in the home, there will be order in the nation. When there is order in the nation, there will be peace in the world."

This philosophy is both simple and profound.

Simple means "not complex or complicated, as a machine of simple construction." I believe you will agree that most of us appreciate some things that are simple and easy to understand, such as truth and integrity. The word *profound* means "deep, descending, or being far below the surface, not superficial." *Profound* also means "humble," as in a profound reverence for the Supreme Being. That certainly gives us something to think about, doesn't it?

~

People today are both geographically and economically ignorant. This must be true because we constantly hear people say, "Where did all my money go?"

Elizabeth Loved Oscar

Love is a game that two can play—and both can win.

The fact that Elizabeth loved Oscar might not sound like headline material, but for me it is. Elizabeth is my special granddaughter. She was born with mental retardation and life holds many challenges for her. One particularly frustrating challenge has been an absolute terror of dogs. Just the barking of a dog could send her screaming. It got so bad that Elizabeth would not go on walks in the neighborhood because of dogs behind fences. She was becoming more and more uncomfortable in the world.

A real breakthrough came the day she saw and held Oscar, a little longhaired, miniature dachshund. Weighing in at under two pounds, Elizabeth saw no threat in this tiny pup. She was delighted and we were thrilled, so we gave Oscar to Elizabeth for her birthday. A few weeks later, our daughter Cindy Oates and her large golden retriever therapy dog, Emmitt, began working with Elizabeth in pet therapy. Cindy's first goal was to get Elizabeth comfortable enough with Emmitt to touch him. This she accomplished in short order and

Elizabeth is now comfortable around Emmitt and the majority of other dogs as well.

The quality of Elizabeth's life has improved considerably because of these two dogs, and she is not unique. All over the country, pets—and particularly dogs—are helping children, adults, and the elderly through pet therapy. Pet therapy is one of the fastest growing fields in America and the demand for dogs and adults to work with them far exceeds the supply. Today the objective of visits by trained therapy dogs in various hospital settings is to help patients do things they haven't been able to do because of an accident, an addiction, or a trauma of some kind.

It's true that others can give you pleasure, but happiness comes when you do things for other people. If your time permits, get involved in a pet therapy program.

~

One reason a dog can be such a comfort when you're feeling blue is that he doesn't try to find out why.

I'm C2 and Fat-Free

Remember, happiness doesn't depend upon who you are or what you have. It depends solely on what you think.

—DALE CARNEGIE

Several years ago I heard about a fellow who returned a phone call and when the phone was answered the response was, "286-7495." The gentleman replied, "Yes, I'm returning Mr. Anderson's call," and the operator said, "Who is this?" He responded, "233-9191."

It seems to be true that many people have become mere numbers in our noncaring, technological world. This was brought home to me recently when I checked in at the gate for one of my numerous flights. When I showed my ticket with the boarding pass to the gate agent, he picked up his microphone and said to the flight attendant aboard, "C2 is here." What he meant was simply that I had seat C2 and was at the gate. I kind of laughed and said to the fellow, "Well, that's the first time I've been identified as a seat number." He smiled as I walked aboard the airplane where I sat down and we took off. When mealtime came, the flight attendant began listing the menu choices for the passengers. When he got to me I said, "I believe I have a special meal." He turned to another attendant and said, "Fat-free is here." Since I prefer to be called Zig, I'm glad the names C2 and Fat-free did not stick.

I find it amusing and yet, in a strange way, a little sad that we've reached that point in life when we can so casually deal with one another as a number or a letter. That's especially true at this time in our history when mergers, downsizing, rightsizing, buyouts, early retirement, and bankruptcy have created stress and fear in the marketplace. Today, people need hope and encouragement, combined with genuine care and concern from those with whom we deal on a regular basis. When we pay our bills with a check or credit card, we like to be called by name. I'm not "C2" and "Fat-free," I'm a human being—and so are you. Let's treat each other that way.

～

Understand that anybody who is somebody to anybody is somebody.

Up in Smoke

Failure should be our teacher, not our undertaker.
Failure is delay—not defeat. It is a temporary detour,
not a dead-end street.

—JOHN MAXWELL

Recently, I saw two attractive teenage girls smoking cigarettes. It was obvious that they were new smokers. As a father who has watched two of his daughters go through the pains of death trying to quit smoking, I wanted to give the two young women a warning and a lecture. I didn't do it, because they could rightfully have said it was none of my business. As an employer, I looked at those two girls and knew that it would definitely jeopardize their opportunities for getting some jobs. Many companies do not hire smokers. I looked at them as future parents and knew what that smoke would do to their babies, should they continue to smoke and ever become mothers.

As a member of a family of twelve with only three remaining siblings, it was tempting to explain to the two girls that all the members of my family who smoked are now dead. The difference between the life spans of the smokers and the nonsmokers is nineteen years—and if the three surviving members of the family live the life span their ages and general health now predict, the difference in life span will be twenty-plus years.

Yes, I was tempted to intercede, but I didn't. Surely there is something responsible citizens can do to intervene with the tobacco industry and force them out of business. Do we really have to watch another generation of children go up in smoke?

Politicians must be made to realize that it is immoral to accept contributions from tobacco companies, that we must someday pay for the atrocities we're committing today on Third World countries by shipping our cigarettes to them by the billions. Our tobacco will kill more of them than all of the cocaine and heroin that is coming into our country from their nations. Talk about hypocrisy, or "the kettle calling the pot black," we need to seriously examine our own values here in this great country. This is truly an international outrage.

~

If you want to keep teenagers out of hot water, just put dirty dishes in it.

A Strange Way to
Show Love

*It is not necessary that we should all think exactly
alike, but we should all think.*

The giraffe is the largest mammal that gives birth to
its young while standing up. I don't speak "giraffe," but
I can imagine what the baby giraffe must be thinking
when he bounces on the ground from that great height.
He just left warm, cushioned quarters in which all his
needs, comforts, and security were provided. Now he
finds himself bouncing off (comparatively speaking)
hard, cold, unwelcoming ground.

Almost immediately thereafter, a new trauma occurs
in the baby giraffe's life. As he struggles to his knees,
Mama Giraffe gets busy "persuading" him to stand up.
She does this as he wobbles to his feet by giving him a
swift kick to prod him to faster action. No sooner does
he reach his feet than Mama delivers a booming kick
that knocks the baby giraffe back down.

Again, I don't speak "giraffe," but I can well imagine the baby giraffe thinking, *Well, make up your
mind, Mom! First you kicked me to make me stand up.
Then you kicked me back down!* Interestingly enough,

once the baby giraffe is back on the ground, Mama Giraffe again starts kicking and nudging until he stands back up.

That process is repeated several times because Mama Giraffe loves her baby. Or is it instinct? Who can say with certainty? However, this we know for certain: Baby Giraffe is a prime delicacy for carnivorous animals, which are a part of his environment. Mama Giraffe knows that the only chance of survival for her baby is to be able to quickly get up and move out of harm's way. Yes, kicking the baby up and down seems like a strange way to show love. But for a baby giraffe it is the ultimate expression of love. Caution: That approach definitely won't work in the "people" world, but the principle will. Real love is evidenced when you do what is best for the other person, whether or not they appreciate it at that moment.

❧

They say it can't be done, but sometimes that doesn't always work. (Baseball legend Casey Stengel in EXECUTIVE SPEECHWRITER NEWSLETTER)

The Young Persuader

The best gifts are wrapped in love and tied with heartstrings.

A few days after my second daughter was born, I had to take a trip over to South Carolina from our Knoxville, Tennessee, home. On the way back, a sudden snowstorm left me and a few hundred other motorists stranded for the night. Fortunately, I was stranded directly behind a nice, warm Greyhound bus. The driver was kind enough to permit me to climb aboard and spend the night. The next morning the highways were cleared and I drove on home.

I had no sooner pulled into the driveway and gotten inside the house than my wife said we needed more baby supplies. I slipped my heavy coat back on and was headed for the door when my soon-to-be four-year-old daughter, Suzan, said, "Daddy, take me with you." I explained to her that the weather was bad, I would only be gone a few minutes, and it would be best for her to stay home. As only a four-year-old can, she said, "But, Daddy, I will be so lonely." I said, "Now, Doll, your mother is here and so is your new baby sister, and Lizzie (who was our live-in nanny) is here." Then she looked at me and said, "But, Daddy, I'll be lonely for you." I don't need to tell you that she went with me to the store that day.

In retrospect, that is persuasion at its absolute best—straight from the heart, without guile and without any subterfuge. In a direct, simple way she made me feel important—I was the one she was going to be lonely for. I believe that if we will play it straight, speak from the heart, and be open and direct with people in a loving way, we will improve our communication skills dramatically and our persuasiveness will go up.

~

No person ever ended his eyesight by looking on the bright side.

The Ultimate Optimist

*Personality has the power to open doors, but it takes
character to keep them open.*

Most people consider me an optimist because I
laughingly state that I would take my last two dollars
and buy a money belt. I'd even go after Moby Dick in a
rowboat, and take the tartar sauce with me! However,
I've got to confess that I don't hold a candle to the ultimate lady optimist who lived in a retirement home. One
day, a distinguished-looking gentleman also became a
resident. As luck would have it, the first day they sat
across the table from each other at lunch. After a few
minutes he grew uncomfortable because she was staring
intently at him. He finally expressed his discomfort and
queried her as to why she was staring. She responded
that she was staring because he reminded her so much
of her third husband—same demeanor, same smile,
same height, weight—everything. The gentleman
replied in some shock, "Third husband! How many
times have you been married?" The lady smilingly said,
"Twice." Yup. That's optimism!

I've got to confess I'm a pragmatic optimist myself.

I love the story of the gentleman who was being given a tour of the Mann Center for the Performing Arts in Tel Aviv. The tour guide was pointing out the features of the incredible structure. The stonework was unbelievably beautiful. The wall tapestries, paintings, and gold inlays were absolutely gorgeous. Finally, the tourist said, "I assume you named the facility for Horace Mann, the famous author." The tour guide answered with a smile, "No, we named it after Frederick Mann from Philadelphia." The tourist remarked, "Frederick Mann? What did he write?" The tour guide said, "A check." Now, that's being pragmatic!

It might interest you to know that the 1828 *Noah Webster Dictionary* identifies the optimist in complimentary terms, but says nothing about the pessimist. The word *pessimist* was not in our vocabulary at that time. It's a modern "invention" that I believe we should "dis-invent." I encourage you to become an optimist—a pragmatic one, that is.

≈

The time to make friends is before you need them.

Three Sides to the Story

Your unhappiness is not due to your want of a for-
tune or high position or fame or sufficient vitamins.
It is due not to a want of something outside of you,
but to a want of something inside you. You were
made for perfect happiness. No wonder everything
short of God disappoints you.

—FULTON SHEEN

My mother often said, "There are three sides to every story—your side, their side, and the right side." Over the years, I have come to the conclusion that in most cases she was right. How often, when we hear the first account of a story, does it appear that someone is guilty without doubt? Later we get the "other side of the story," and completely change our minds. "Don't rush to judgment" is good advice.

A typical example is something that took place at our company recently. An employee reported an incident to me in which he was not directly involved but had heard about "through the grapevine." The evidence seemed compelling that a serious error in judgment by a key staff member had occurred. However, after talking with those directly involved, who had all the relevant information, the picture changed dramatically.

As it developed, there were three sides. Each was right, but critical information was incomplete. This led to the erroneous original conclusion that a serious error had been made. What was needed was that old Paul Harvey standby, "the rest of the story," which validated the fact that there were three sides.

I encourage you, particularly if you're in a management or decision-making position regarding other people, to carefully hear what the messenger is saying. Make no decisions, promises, or judgments until you have heard the other side of the story. Take that approach and you'll win more friends and influence more people.

~

Most people who berate their luck never think to question their judgment.

Dad, You *Do* Choose Your Daughter's Husband

If what you believe doesn't affect how you live, then it isn't very important.

—DICK NOGLEBERG

Don't misunderstand. I'm not suggesting that you go through the newspaper or the neighborhood, selecting the husband you believe would be appropriate for your daughter. But I would like to point out that you *do* help your daughter select her future husband. The process starts when your little girl is happily sitting on your knee or riding your back. The truth is, the first knowledge our daughters acquire about relationships with the opposite sex comes from their fathers. What you teach your daughter about how men treat women becomes the cornerstone of her expectations. If you treat your wife with courtesy and respect, your daughter will file that in her memory bank as the way she should be treated by her future husband.

When your daughter sees you loving her mother and treating her with respect, she comes to know that men should treat their wives that way. However, if your daughter sees you abuse her mother, she learns that's the way men treat women and so she's not surprised—though she obviously doesn't like it—if her husband abuses her. This is especially true if it happens in small steps during the courtship process and gradually gets worse once she is married.

When we got married, one of the things my wife's mother told her was, "You've made a lifetime deal, but if he ever abuses you, you've got a home you can come to." By the strangest of coincidences, that's what we told our children. This communication to one of our daughters possibly helped her—and us—avoid a tragic mistake.

So, Dad, all this really says is that if you love your little girl, you will treat her and her mother with respect and dignity. If you do, chances are excellent your daughter will choose her husband wisely. In fact, he will probably be just like the guy old Dad would have chosen.

~

Vanity—People should not forget the mama whale's advice to her baby: "Remember, it is only when you spout off that you get harpooned."

Here's Why I'm a
Boy Scout Fan

The best index to a person's character is (a) how he
treats people who can't do him any good and (b) how
he treats people who can't fight back.

On September 26, 1993, fifteen-year-old B. J. Russell
of Spokane, Washington, and his dad, Don, along with
a friend, Dave Hibb, were riding motorcycles. They
were riding single file at 5 miles an hour on a deeply rut-
ted back road. Dave was bringing up the rear. Suddenly,
B. J. and his dad heard a loud thump, followed by a cry
of pain. Dave had hit a rut and fallen over. His bike was
on top of him, still running and leaking gasoline. B. J.
lifted the bike off and found that Dave's left kneecap
was seriously dislocated and was going into spasms
from the intense pain. At that point, B. J.'s dad started
the forty-five-minute trip to retrieve Dave's truck. While
he was gone, using techniques he learned in Boy Scouts,
B. J. splinted Dave's injured leg. He used fallen branches
and a piece of rope he had with him, causing the
kneecap to return to its correct position. He then helped
Dave out of the middle of the road, gave him some
water, and calmed him down as best he could. Later, at

the hospital, the doctor said that Dave's knee had already been reset, thanks to B. J.'s splinting.

The fascinating part of the story is the fact that here was a fun outing with a father, son, and friend thoroughly enjoying themselves. When the accident occurred, thanks to what he had learned in Scouting, B. J. was able to do what was necessary to relieve some pain and speed the return of the knee to a healthy status more quickly, thus reducing the time required for rehabilitation.

In this day and time it's exciting to know that both one- and two-parent families have a place they can go to find a marvelous role model for enjoyment and character development for their kids. Think about it and if you have a youngster in the age bracket of nine to eighteen, get involved in Scouting.

~

A vacationist caught a fish so big he dislocated both shoulders describing it.

Try It—Maybe You Can

Everyone hears only what he understands.

—GOETHE

I love the story of the ninety-year-old lady who, when asked if she could play the piano, responded that she didn't know. "What do you mean, you don't know?" she was asked. The lady smilingly replied, "I've never tried." That's a good answer that I hope will open some eyes, ears, and thinking. Many of us have talents we've never benefited from because we have never "tried" to do a specific thing.

Nearly everybody recognizes the name of Nat "King" Cole. He was universally admired for his beautiful, silky-smooth voice. He could sing ballads as few have ever done. What many people do not realize is that he started his career as a piano player. One night in a West Coast club, the featured singer was ill and the owner demanded to know where he was. When Cole responded that he was sick, the club owner said, "If we don't have a singer there'll be no check." That night Nat "King" Cole became a singer. The rest is history.

For the first seven years of his career, Will Rogers

performed rope tricks. He was a genuine cowboy and very much a "man's man." He held the attention of the audience with the rope tricks he performed. One night someone in the audience asked him a question. His candid response brought a considerable amount of laughter. Then someone else asked a question and Rogers's response again was humorous. That night his career as a full-scale humorist was launched. But he was far more than a humorist. He had the homespun wisdom that not only encouraged and entertained, but also gave people information and inspiration they could use in their everyday lives.

Message: You might not be able to carry a tune, do rope tricks, or give humorous, homespun advice, but you do have a song to sing and ability that needs to be developed and used.

Suggestion: The next time someone asks if you can do something you've never done before, don't automatically respond "no." Think about it. Maybe you should give it a try. Who knows? Maybe you have talents you've never recognized.

∾

In the town I was raised in things moved so slowly it took two hours to watch Sixty Minutes. (KEN DAVIS)

That First Impression

He who gains a victory over other men is strong, but he who gains a victory over himself is all-powerful.

—LAO-TZU

It's true that you only have one chance to make a first impression. Despite this fact, American business is rife with receptionists who are neither pleasant, courteous, upbeat, or even understandable. Many companies apparently feel that anybody can "answer the telephone." While it is true that anyone can be taught the mechanics of answering the telephone, lasting impressions are made—especially on first-time callers—of the type of company you have by the way that phone is answered.

Very recently we received an exciting letter from one of our suppliers. The gentleman is the director of sales for his corporation. He commented with considerable enthusiasm that when he phoned our company he first got Lou and then on the second call, Barbara answered. His verbatim comment was this: "Sir, I must tell you I have worked telephones for the majority of my adult life and never have I heard phones answered in such an upbeat and pleasant manner. If the first voices you hear at a company are your first impressions of a company, you, sir, have a first-class company. You are to be congratulated on the quality and training of your personnel."

I mention this not to "toot our own horn," but simply to remind you that every time the phone rings at your company (or your home), it is an opportunity for someone to make either a good or a poor impression. Needless to say, you build business with good impressions. It's true that you have to follow through with the rest of it, but the start is important. In our computerized hurry-hurry world, I strongly urge you to train your people to assume that the next caller is the biggest account your company might ever land and they need to be pleasant, cheerful, courteous, and enthusiastic.

~

Teacher to parent: "The good news is your child has a lot of creative ideas . . . The bad news is they are all in spelling."

Persistence and a
Good Heart = Success

Not in the clamor of the crowded street, nor in the shouts and plaudits of the throng, but in ourselves are triumph and defeat.

—HENRY WADSWORTH LONGFELLOW

As a young man, Joe Craven had an idea to start a pottery manufacturing business. He built an advanced kiln but could not make it work. He tried time after time and finally conceded failure. Then he got on his knees and asked for help. By "coincidence," the next morning two gentlemen from Texas who had heard about his kiln asked to see it. Joe reluctantly agreed but told them it didn't work. One commented that he had just returned from a tour in Germany where they were using this technology but he was surprised to see it in the United States. He shared some procedures he had learned and Joe agreed to give their concept a try. It worked! Today, Craven Pottery, located in Commerce, Georgia, does over $35 million in business yearly and has 320 employees.

In the summer of 1994, Doug Segars, the assistant manager at Craven Pottery, got an offer he couldn't refuse from another company. He had been with Craven for many years but felt this was an opportunity to advance his career.

Joe Craven gave him a good-bye party and he departed with the blessings and encouragement of all. Two days before he was to leave for the new home, Doug's wife and two daughters were hit head-on in an automobile accident. One of his daughters was seriously injured and was in a coma for three weeks.

Joe knew that the tragedy had probably knocked Doug out of his new opportunity, so he told Doug and his family that no matter what happened, Doug would have a job at Craven when it was all over. Today, Doug is functioning as the Sales Coordinator at Craven Pottery. Because Joe had eased his mind about his economic future, Doug was able to direct his attention to his first priority, his family. Neat to know, isn't it, that we still have some "good guys" left in the world. Good guys (and good girls) really do win.

～

You're not finished when you're defeated, you're finished when you quit.

Why You Are Where You Are

Choice—not chance—determines human destiny.

Many years ago as a young, aspiring speaker, I heard an older speaker who was quite philosophical say that you are where you are because that's exactly where you want to be. I thought about his statement, decided it was the "wisdom of the ages," and verbalized it in my own presentations. Over a period of time, a series of events took place that convinced me his statement was not true in my case. I was broke, in debt, and down in the dumps. I wanted to be prosperous and excited about my future.

It came through loud and clear that I was where I was and what I was because of the decisions and choices I had made in my life. I made those choices based on the information I had, much of which was erroneous. The reality is, if I'm given the wrong directions to go from "Point A" to "Point B," I'm not going to reach Point B unless I change directions. It's equally true that if I'm given the wrong directions on how to move from being broke and in debt to being successful and prosperous, I'm not going to end up at the place I want to be.

One important decision you can make even as you read these words is to think about what Thomas Sikking said: "You're not the product of a broken home, a devastated economy, a world in the upheaval of war, a minority group, a family of drunkards, or a poverty-ridden neighborhood. You are the product of your own thinking processes and whatever you're thinking about today is the cornerstone of your tomorrow."

If someone else has abused you in the past, it's okay to give them credit for fouling up your past, but do not give them permission to ruin your present and your future. Take control of your thoughts and your future. Determine that you will have a better tomorrow.

~

Being popular is important; otherwise people might not like you. (SUE CANTWELL)

The Window of Opportunity

There is an advantage in every disadvantage and a gift in every problem.

—JOHN JOHNSON

On Saturday, June 24, 1995, I was in Tampa, Florida, for a seminar. At seven o'clock I stepped out of my hotel to do my walking but, unfortunately, it was raining. The good news is that there was a parking garage attached to the hotel, so I headed there to take my walk. Needless to say, I prefer to walk outdoors where I can see things as I go, but walking in a covered garage beats getting wet, and certainly beats not walking at all. I had been enjoying my walk and planning my talk for about twenty-five minutes when I suddenly noticed that the rain had stopped. I hurried outside to take advantage of that window of opportunity and had made it about a block and a half when the rain returned. I headed back to the covered garage and continued my walk—and the planning of my talk.

As I reflect on my activity that morning, I had no idea how long it would continue to rain or how long the break in the rain would last. However, I do believe that too many people wait for everything to be "just right" before they do anything, and they often miss out on life's opportunities.

The second little lesson I learned on that walk is that in a parking garage you follow the incline to the top. It's more difficult to walk up, but to develop endurance you've got to go uphill. To go up in the business world or, for that matter, in the academic or political world, you frequently have to experience difficulty as you go. Without the difficulty you never develop the mental sharpness and physical strength necessary to succeed.

Somebody once said that the only way to the mountaintop is through the valley. When you encounter those "mountains," just remember that the climbing will enable you to climb the next one higher and faster.

∽

They say money doesn't go far these days, but it sure manages to keep its distance from me! (CURRENT COMEDY)

The Heart of a Champion

It's not what the vision is, it's what the vision does.

Some things cannot be measured, and the heart is one of them. I think of three current and former NFL stars. Mike Singletary, according to the experts, was too short and his 40-yard speed was not that great. However, they could not measure his heart and they did not measure his speed for the first five to fifteen yards, and at that distance he was exceptionally fast. As a result, when a running back would break through the line of scrimmage, instead of stopping him five to eight yards downfield as most linebackers do, Singletary was able to stop him in the first couple of yards. That made quite a difference.

Emmitt Smith's 40-yard speed was not earth-shattering, either, and that caused him to be drafted later than he otherwise would have been. Again, the experts could not measure his heart nor the burst of speed he was able to generate from the instant he touched the ball. As a result of both, he was able to break through the hole at the line and pick up those five to eight yards on a consistent basis and frequently break for much longer runs.

Jerry Rice is the other classic example. His 40-yard speed also was not record-breaking, but his commitment to excellence and the fact that he was a game-player, meaning that once the chips were down he was at his best, were not measurable. Videotape of Jerry Rice shows him running stride for stride downfield with a defensive back until the pass is thrown to him. At that point, Jerry turns on the afterburners and frequently leaves the defensive back well behind.

There's something here for all of us to learn. Namely, we can measure I.Q., speed, strength, and a host of other things, but the will to win and the commitment to excellence will enable a person of average ability to excel. So, use what you've got—including your heart.

~

You can't just go on being a good egg . . . you must either hatch or go bad.

Listen to the Coach

The philosopher Aristotle described "power" as the ability to make things be.

If you ask virtually any coach what they look for in an athlete, he or she will go down a list that will include talent, physical strength, skill, and the right mental attitude. Then they will proceed to elaborate on the last one, because the right mental attitude involves a number of things. At the top of that list is the willingness to be coached.

The young athlete who aspires to greatness, generally speaking, learns a number of things from several different coaches. The first one taught him the fundamentals; the second one instilled discipline in him and taught him more of the techniques that must be mastered to excel. Finally, there is the coach who had the rare ability to spot the athlete's unique talent and then maximize that talent by teaching proper techniques.

The one thing coaches cannot tolerate—and the good ones don't—is the individual who grows arrogant because he excelled at a lower level and believes he has nothing else to learn. The good coaches recognize that some things cannot be coached. However, the coach clearly understands that regardless of the extent of the talent, it can be more completely utilized if the proper coaching technique is applied. That coaching technique will include teaching the athletes to become team players by fitting their individual talents into the team. That's significant, because there is a dramatic difference between an all-star team and a team of all-stars. The coach's job is to take the stars and make them a team. The athlete who won't be coached simply never moves up to that last level, which is necessary for maximum personal performance and a must if the athlete is going to be a major contributor to the success of the team.

The blending of this talent into the "team" applies in any family, business, orchestra, stage production, or any other organization of more than two people. Think about it. Listen to the "coach."

~

To exercise is human . . . not to is divine. (CURRENT COMEDY)

Look at the Other Side

When a man won't listen to his conscience, it's usually because he doesn't want advice from a total stranger.

Abraham Lincoln, truly one of our greatest presidents, had a rather unique approach in trying a case when he was a practicing attorney. He went to great lengths to learn everything he could about what the attorney for the "other side" would say and the evidence he would present. Then, in his arguments, Lincoln would do a superb job of presenting the case from his opponent's side of the table. He was complimentary without being condescending. He gave the factual side from the other person's perspective. He even brought their feelings and their beliefs into play. On occasion, the attorney for the other side would make the observation that Lincoln had presented the opposition's case better than he could have.

Perhaps you wonder why he took such an approach. First, he wanted to be fair. Second, he wanted to win the case if he believed his client was right. Needless to say, Lincoln then presented his own side with more fervor, facts, and reasons why his side was the right side. By using this procedure, Lincoln completely robbed the opposition of anything to say and built his own case in a stronger manner. That's one reason Lincoln won so many cases. He also wove in more humor and homespun stories when he presented his case. Most people, including jurors, like and trust those who give them cause to smile and who bring homespun logic to the table.

What Lincoln did was simple. He practiced great human relations and used his abundant common sense. He wanted right to prevail and when he presented his case, as a general rule, the right side did win.

～

Originality is forgetting where you got it.

The Bull's-Eye Is "Hit-Able"

Those who have earned the right to boast don't have to.

Somebody once said that the major difference between a big shot and a little shot is that the big shot was the little shot who kept on shooting. There's much truth in that witticism. The reality is, no matter what our target might be, we seldom hit it on the first try unless the target is low, which means the accomplishment—and the rewards—will be insignificant.

In bow shooting, experienced archers will test the wind by using the first shot to judge its strength and direction, enabling them to zero in on the target with their following shots. In short, archers learn from their mistakes. That's good advice for all of us.

Success in business, athletics, science, politics, or any other endeavor seldom comes on the first effort. Walt Disney went bankrupt a number of times and had at least one nervous breakdown before he made it big. Athletic skills are acquired over a long period of time and after countless hours of practice. Authors by the hundreds can tell you stories by the thousands of those rejection slips before they found a publisher who was willing to "gamble" on an unknown. It's more than just a cliché that persistent, enthusiastic effort produces powerful, positive results, that failure is an event—not a person—and that the only time you must not fail is the last time you try.

Whatever your target might be, chances are good that you're not going to hit the bull's-eye on the first effort you make at being "successful." The key is persistence and the willingness to try again in the face of those early misses. You can learn from those early mistakes and if you do keep on shooting, it's just a question of time before you, too, are hitting the bull's-eye.

∼

I have to put off some things several times before they slip my mind.

Most Men Don't Understand

It's not your position in life—it's the disposition you have which will change your position.

—DR. DAVID MCKINLEY

It's true. The typical husband and father doesn't have a clue as to what the housewife—whether she be full-time or part-time—does to maintain the home. Ruth Hampton expressed it this way: "The most influential position in the nation today is held by a woman. She enforces law, practices medicine, and teaches without degree, certificate of competence, or required training. She handles the nation's food, administers its drugs, and practices emergency first aid. She cares for all the physical and mental ills of the family; a man literally places his life and the lives of his children in the hands of this woman—his wife."

It is, of course, true that many men—and, fortunately, this is increasing, though it's still far from equal—do help with things around the house. However, there is a tremendous difference between helping and being responsible for. Typically, the husband asks "What can I do?" when the wife can clearly see what needs to be done. The husband, too, often assumes that it's "no big deal," that his wife really doesn't need any help, and besides, he needs to relax after a tough day. Example: On Monday night, even though she might be as much a football fan as her husband, she's the one who puts the laundry into the washer, moves it to the dryer during the commercial break, and folds and places the clothes where they belong at halftime. When the game is over, if she's had any interest in it, she probably takes the dishes out of the dishwasher. In the meantime, the husband doesn't have a clue as to what's going on. There is a significant difference between taking responsibility and offering to help.

Now, husbands, before you get too upset with me, remember, if the shoe doesn't fit, don't wear it. However, studies reveal that what I've said is largely true.

~

Husband to frustrated wife: "Remember, dear, you must cultivate patience because the hand that rocks the cradle rules the world." Young mother: "Then you come in here, my dear, and rule the world for a while. I'm tired."

Communicating Effectively

It's not what you know or whom you know. It's what you are that finally counts.

My friend, author-speaker Nido Qubein, in his *Executive Briefing* newsletter, gives some advice on communicating with people from other cultures. "We must remember that people from different backgrounds send and receive messages through cultural filters. Words, expressions, and gestures that mean one thing in one culture may mean something entirely different in another culture. A term or a gesture that may seem perfectly harmless to you may be offensive to someone from another ethnic group." Nido says that "we must first find out what terms and expressions are offensive to minority ears and avoid slang words that refer to people of different racial, ethnic, or national minorities. Don't use them even in joking. Next, we need to understand that English is a precise language but is perceived as blunt by many speakers of other languages. For example, Americans often pride themselves on 'telling it like it is,' but this is a turnoff to Japanese workers who practice 'ishin-den-shin'—that is, communication by the heart."

"Saving face" is an important consideration in some cultures, and this may influence the way people respond to you. If you say, "Do you understand?" to someone from an Asian culture, you may get a polite "yes" when the person has no idea what you're talking about. If they say "no," it can only mean one of two things to many Asians: They're too dense to comprehend or you are a poor instructor. Nido says that it's important to watch the facial expressions of the person with whom we're talking. It's hard to disguise puzzlement and it's usually easy enough to tell whether the face comprehends. He suggests that first of all we ask for feedback; second, that we listen carefully for questions because if there are no questions, there's likely to be no understanding. Third, we should use clear, simple language. This is only a minute capsule of communicating properly with those from other cultures, but it's a good place to start.

~

Women cry when watching a weepy melodrama for the same reason men yell and scream when a man they don't know hits a home run.

Most of Us Are Parrots

Without integrity no one listens. Without trust no one follows.

In our society today we hear clichés and repeat them, whether they make sense or not. For example, Shakespeare said, "Nothing is either good or bad, but thinking makes it so." A moment's reflection will convince you that thinking has nothing to do with whether rape or murder is good or bad. Those acts are bad. Many people today say, "Well, everything is relative," which is also absurd. We must have some absolutes in life; otherwise, obeying the law is "relative." There are several thousand laws on the books, so let's go down the list and choose the ones that are relative to us and, consequently, obey only them. Chaos would be the obvious result.

For the eighty-five-year-old, driving 40 miles per hour might seem far too fast, while 90 miles per hour for the seventeen-year-old might not seem fast at all. A "bump" by a 300-pound NFL offensive lineman on a 290-pound defensive end would be relatively insignificant. The same force applied against a frail senior citizen could result in serious consequences.

As you ponder things of this nature, I believe you will come to the conclusion that the more things we make relative, the more chaos we're going to have in our society. It's safe to say that virtually every husband and wife in America does not want their mate to be "relatively" faithful. Most of us have even taken vows that being relative has nothing to do with. We're going to love, cherish, honor, and be faithful to our spouse. Add relativity and good or bad to that vow, and very few marriages would survive.

The list is endless, but I encourage you to eliminate much of this "relativity stuff," and this idea that "nothing is either good or bad but thinking makes it so" approach to life. Follow the moral absolutes that have stood civilization in good stead for several thousand years.

~

Why is it that what you hear is never quite as interesting as what you overhear?

Don't Always Take
It Literally

*The bridges you've crossed before you come to them
are over rivers that aren't there.*

—GENE BROWN

My trusty dictionary tells me that the word *literal* means "according to the letter; primitive, real, not figurative or metaphorical, as the literal meaning of a phrase."

As a cub reporter, Mark Twain was told never to state as fact anything that he could not personally verify. Because he was the person he was, he decided to take those instructions literally and he wrote about a social event in this manner: "A woman, giving the name of Mrs. James Jones, who is reported to be one of the society leaders of the city, is said to have given what purported to be a party yesterday to a number of alleged ladies. The hostess claims to be the wife of a reputed attorney."

Recently, I was getting my regular eye examination from my friend and ophthalmologist, Dr. Nathan Lipton, who has quite a unique sense of humor. As we moved through the various stages of the examination, he told me to cover my left eye, which I did. A few seconds later he said, "Now, cover your right eye," and I proceeded to cover my right eye without removing my left hand from my left eye. Needless to say, that's not exactly what Dr. Lipton had in mind, but we both broke out laughing.

The truth is, many times when someone tells us something they expect us to use a little common sense in listening to and hearing what they say. Have a little fun as you go through life. Take some things to be literally true and act accordingly—the chuckle you get out of it will brighten your day and help someone else feel happier, too.

~

Definition: A pedestrian is someone who was certain there was gas in the tank, even though the gauge registered empty. (PETER ELDIN)

Positive Trivia

Character is the total of thousands of small daily strivings to live up to the best that is in us.
— LT. GEN. A. G. TROUDEAU

Some people are quick to condemn clichés but what is a cliché? It is a truth that has retained its validity through time. Mankind would lose much of its hard-earned wisdom, built up patiently over the ages, if it ever lost its clichés.

A lie may take care of the present, but it definitely has no future.

Tact is the art of recognizing when to be big and when not to belittle.

Whoever acquires knowledge but doesn't practice it is like the one who plows a field but doesn't sow it.

You can't climb the ladder of success with cold feet.

If you learn only methods you'll be tied to your methods, but if you learn principles you can devise your own methods. (RALPH WALDO EMERSON)

If you would lift me up, you must be on higher ground. (RALPH WALDO EMERSON)

Most of what happens to you happens because of you.

Our words reveal our thoughts and mirror our self-esteem; actions reflect our character, our habits, and predict the future. (WILLIAM ARTHUR WARD)

Tact is the art of building a fire under people without making their blood boil.

Imagination is the preview of life's coming attractions.

All of us are shaped by what others expect of and from us. We live either up or down to what others believe about us and what we can do. Actually, what other people think of us is frequently more crucial and influential than what we think of ourselves. Therefore, we should be careful of our associates because in many ways they will influence what we do with our life.

You've got to believe before you can achieve.

~

A committee is a group of people who individually can do nothing but collectively meet and decide that nothing can be done. (GOV. ALFRED SMITH)

Icing on the Cake

People with low self-esteem find failure so devastating that they seldom take even sensible, calculated risks, and miss out on many of life's joys and successes.

One of the favorite expressions of highly successful and/or competitive people is the phrase, "If such and such a thing happens, that will just be the icing on the cake." A sprinter, for example, might say, "I'm going to try awfully hard to win the race and if, in the process, I break the record, that will be 'icing on the cake.'" A salesperson might say, "My objective is to meet my quota this quarter, and if I win the trip, that will be the 'icing on the cake.'"

Hakeem Olajuwon, the all-pro center for the Houston Rockets, gave a new dimension and thought to that phrase just before the final game in the 1994 championship series with the New York Nicks. The teams were tied at three games each and each game, with one exception, had been decided in the last few seconds of the contest. It was truly one of the great championship series of all time.

Just before the championship game, a reporter

asked Hakeem if his life would be ruined if the Rockets did not win the championship. His answer is an indication of Hakeem's sincerity and humility. "I've seen some guys who did win a championship, but at the end of their careers they weren't happy. To me, that's not a successful career. If you feel joy about what you've accomplished, no matter what profession it is, you've had a successful career. For me the championship would be the icing on the cake, but I'll still have the cake, no matter what. You can look at how far you've come and be happy or you can dwell on where you haven't been and spend your lifetime believing you have been deprived of something. I can't."

Incidentally, *Hakeem* literally means "doctor" or "wise one," and *Olajuwon* means "at the top." His name is reflected in his approach to life.

∼

They can make a machine that can beat you at chess, but does it know it's won? (KEN CAMPBELL, SUNDAY TIMES)

Communicators Listen and Practice

No man ever became great doing as he pleased. Little men do as they please; little nobodies. Great men submit themselves to the laws governing the realm of their greatness.

When you invoke the name of Martin Luther King, an image is painted in the mind of virtually everyone of a truly great leader and a great communicator who was the driving force behind the Civil Rights Movement. Excerpts from his speech, "I Have a Dream," are still aired regularly on television and every schoolchild in America can quote portions of that famous speech.

Everyone who heard him would agree that he was a great speaker, but many do not realize that he was a great communicator because he was an even greater listener. It is said that Martin Luther King gained the respect of the Civil Rights leaders who disagreed with him because he listened so intently to everything they had to say. Feeling secure in his thinking, it made sense to him that it was important to know what they were thinking. Because he listened to them so intently, they extended him the same courtesy and listened carefully to what he had to say. That way each side knew what the other's thinking and planning was, and that gave the movement great force.

The other reason Martin Luther King was such a great communicator was the fact that his "I Have a Dream" speech had been given countless times before he gave it in Washington when it received so much publicity. Had he not done the lengthy and extensive preparation, however, the speech in Washington would not have been nearly as impactive.

Many of the same things could be said about Patrick Henry. His famous "Give Me Liberty or Give Me Death" speech had been given many times before he had the opportunity to present it to the audience, which proved to be the catalyst that ignited the American Revolution.

It has been said that when Cicero spoke the people stood and cheered, but when Demosthenes spoke the people stood and marched. The same thing could be said about Martin Luther King and Patrick Henry. When they spoke, the people marched.

~

"And do you pray every night?" asked the new minister. "No," answered the little boy. "Some nights I don't need nothin'."

Hooray for Krish—Shame on Zig

When you admit you made a mistake and apologize to the offended party, you are simply acknowledging that you are wiser now than you were when you made the mistake.

Recently my associate Krish Dhanam and I were returning from an engagement in Tampa, Florida, where we had spoken for the Greater Tampa Chamber of Commerce. The flight was uneventful; we landed at the Dallas–Fort Worth airport, got our luggage and loaded it on one of the rental carts. The walk was fairly lengthy and the first two hundred yards were uneventful; then we came to the moving sidewalks.

The rules regarding carts on moving sidewalks are fairly clear—you just don't do it. Krish, pushing the cart, dutifully headed for the side and I laughingly said, "Krish, on Saturday they waive the rule. It's okay to take the cart on the moving sidewalk." A nearby flight attendant said, "No, it's against the rules." Krish appeared hesitant but I encouraged him, "Aw, come on, Krish, nobody else is on, let's do it." Krish is from India. His culture, background, and training, and the fact that

I was his "boss," created a dilemma. He knew the rules, but he respected me. He therefore complied with my rather insistent suggestion that we use the moving sidewalk.

Once we got on the conveyor I sensed that Krish was having a real struggle, so at the first break in the walk I laughingly told Krish that it would be okay for him to do what he wanted to do and walk alongside the moving sidewalk. With a noticeable look of relief, he did exactly that.

The purpose of this story is not to tell you about my misdeeds, but to emphasize one reason legal immigrants, regardless of where they're from, are four times as likely to become millionaires in America as are those who are born here. Their gratitude for the opportunity and freedom America offers is such that most of them are very conscientious about obeying our laws. As a result, these legal immigrants make real progress in achieving the American Dream.

≈

The trouble with ignorance is that it picks up confidence as it goes along.

This Is Real Leadership

Be a gift-giver. To all men give charity; to yourself, respect; to a friend, your heart; to your father, deference; to your child, a good example; to a personal enemy, forgiveness; to your mother, conduct that will make her proud of you.

On Saturday, October 7, 1995, Eddie Robinson, the now-retired head football coach of Grambling State University in Ruston, Louisiana, led his team to its four-hundredth victory, a mark never before reached that probably will not be reached again. That's exciting. Even more exciting, however, is the approach "Coach Rob"—as his players called him with great affection and respect—used to see to it that his players got their degrees. He was the last one to leave the dorm in the morning, making certain that every player was on his way to class. He checked regularly to make certain they were doing their academic work. He required them to wear coats and ties when being interviewed by the media. He took them to classes in etiquette and taught them manners and how to deal with people. In simple terms, Coach Rob was preparing his players for life, knowing that most of them, as is true in all other schools, would not make it to the pros.

I became an Eddie Robinson fan several years ago when I turned on the television to catch the news but instead saw Coach Rob's team playing a game that would ultimately determine the national small college championship. It was close and hard-fought. One of the most decisive plays was a field goal the other team made, though it clearly had not split the uprights. Coach Rob knew this, as did every television viewer in America and every football player involved, but the officials would not relent. When the game was over, Coach Rob did not mention that decisive mistake on the part of the officials. I'm certain he was terribly disappointed and very upset, but he put it in perspective, realizing that a missed field goal, when mingled with millions of incidents that happen in our lifetime, really was not that important. Setting an example for his players and teaching them about real success was important. He's a class act.

~

Fans, don't fail to miss tomorrow's game. (DIZZY DEAN)

Be a People Person

When enthusiasm is inspired by reason, controlled by caution, sound in theory, practical in application, reflects confidence, spreads good cheer, raises morale, inspires associates, arouses loyalty, and laughs at adversity, it is beyond price.

—COLEMAN COX

In his inspiring book by that title, John Maxwell tells a story. In England there is a monument to the sport of rugby, the forerunner of American football. The monument depicts an eager boy leaning down to pick up a ball. At the base is this inscription: "With a fine disregard for the rules, he picked up the ball and ran."

The statue and inscription tell a true story. An important game of soccer was taking place between two English schools. During the closing minutes of the contest, a boy, more gifted with enthusiasm and school spirit than with experience, was sent into the game for the first time. Forgetting all the rules, particularly the one that says a player does not touch the ball with his hands, and conscious only of the fact that the ball had to be in the goal within seconds if his school was to be victorious, the boy picked up the ball and, to the amazement of everyone, started the sprint of his life toward the goal. The confused officials and players remained frozen where they stood, but the spectators were so moved by the boy's spirit and entertained by his performance that they stood up and applauded long and loudly. This incident totally eclipsed the rest of the game's action. As a result, a new sport was born: rugby. It wasn't because of carefully worded arguments and rule changes, it was because of one boy's enthusiastic mistake.

The bottom line is that sometimes spontaneity produces incredible results and enthusiasm is always an asset in life.

~

In a Chicago tailor shop: As you rip, so shall we sew.

America Was Populated and Freed by a Salesman

Civilizations do not give out, they give in. In a society where anything goes, eventually everything will.

—JOHN UNDERWOOD

World conditions were horrible when the settlement of America started and people were desperately needed to populate the new, uncharted wilderness. Sir Walter Raleigh toured the coffeehouses of London, persuading people who were living in distress that there was a better land and a better way to live. The people were ignorant, fearful, and superstitious, so it took a lot of selling on Raleigh's part to persuade them to leave the "security" of their homeland.

America was freed by a salesman. George Washington's task to recruit for the Continental army looked insurmountable. He had to convince the farmers, merchants, shipbuilders, fur trappers, and other workmen to stop what they were doing and go to war against the most powerful nation on earth, the one with the dominant navy and a large, professional, well-trained, well-equipped army. He had to tell them if they won the war there would be little, if any, money to pay them, and if they lost the war, they would be hung from the highest trees. Yes, it was a tough sell, but Washington was a salesman on fire for freedom.

America was explored by a salesman. Though America had been discovered in 1492, by 1776, or nearly three hundred years later, it had been settled only as far west as the Appalachian Mountains. However, Secretary of the Treasury Alexander Hamilton persuaded Congress to appropriate money to study the methods the British had used to establish themselves around the world. Trading posts were the result, and Lewis and Clark got their jump start toward reaching the Pacific Coast. In fewer than fifty more years, a strong presence had been established all over this great land.

Yes, the salesperson has played a significant role in our country.

~

According to the government, a taxpayer is someone who has what it takes.

A Bear in a Tree

Concern should drive us into action and not into a depression.

Several years ago at dusk, just outside of Keithville, Louisiana, someone spotted a black bear in a tree. Word quickly spread around the little town and many of the citizens gathered to see him. The local veterinarian provided a dart gun loaded with drugs to sedate him. Concern was raised that the bear might fall out of the tree and injure himself, so the fire department was called and their net was put in place to catch him.

A bonfire was built and all night long they tried to get that bear out of the tree. It seemed he was oblivious to the crowd and apparently the drugs were having no effect on him because no bear came tumbling from the tree.

Then came the dawn and they could more clearly see that "bear" in the tree. The bear turned out to be a black plastic bag, filled with garbage. No one as of yet has figured out how that garbage bag got to the top of the tree.

Unfortunately, many people live with a "bear up

their tree," and allow it to impact their lives in a harmful way. When they learn the truth they discover the "bear" is negative garbage that has been dumped in their mind over a period of time by music, television, and "friends," as well as the general public. The good news is that, regardless of their age, a person can get that "bear" out of their tree by bringing it to the light of day—as they did in Keithville, Louisiana. Simply by reversing the process and putting good, clean, pure, powerful, and positive information into their mind, a person can bury that "old garbage." I've seen numerous people who follow that procedure dramatically improve their lives. You can do the same thing.

~

A big-game hunter today is a fellow who switches channels all Sunday afternoon during football season.

Education Is Important

It's in the struggle itself that you define yourself.

—PAT BUCHANAN

Albert Einstein said, "It is essential that the student acquire an understanding of and a lively feeling for values. He must acquire a vivid sense of the beautiful and of the morally good, otherwise he—with a specialized knowledge—more closely resembles a well-trained dog than a harmoniously developed person." Daniel Webster said, "Knowledge does not comprise all which is contained in the large term of education. The feelings are to be disciplined, the passions are to be restrained, true and worthy motives are to be inspired, a profound religious feeling is to be instilled, and pure morality inculcated under all circumstances. All this is comprised in education."

James Truslow Adams says there are obviously two educations: One should teach us how to make a living and the other how to live. In order to acquire both educations, three things are necessary: We need information, knowledge, and wisdom. We get information out of newspapers and magazines. We acquire knowledge through good books, encyclopedias, lectures, and seminars. But these first two will not give us both types of education. If information and knowledge were the complete answer, every Ph.D. in America would be rich and happy, and every high school dropout would be broke and miserable. Obviously, this is not true.

The third dimension of education is wisdom. Wisdom is the correct use of the truth in the knowledge we have. Wisdom enables us to take information and knowledge and use it to make good decisions. On a personal level, my mother finished only the fifth grade, was widowed in the heart of the Great Depression, and had six children too young to work. Obviously, she needed wisdom to use the knowledge she had to make right decisions to successfully raise her family. Fortunately, she had the wisdom that comes from God, which James speaks of in his epistle: "If any of you lacks wisdom, let him ask of God, who gives to all liberally and without reproach, and it will be given to him" (1:5).

～

There aren't nearly enough crutches in the world for all the lame excuses. (MARCUS STROUP)

114

Is Guilt Good or Bad?

To forgive is to overlook an offense and treat the offender as not guilty.

If you follow trials in our courtrooms on a regular basis, you know that after the judge has passed sentence he will read one of two statements. If the criminal is given a sentence lighter than the crime seemed to warrant, the statement will frequently include the fact that the perpetrator of the crime was genuinely remorseful and had a deep sense of guilt for the wrong done, so the judge believed he or she would not be a threat to society.

On the other hand, if the sentence is the maximum for the crime, the judge, the arresting officers, and others will say the accused had absolutely no remorse, felt no guilt, and "we believe he or she will repeat this crime."

The dictionary says that *guilt* is the "fact of being responsible for an offense or wrongdoing; the disposition to break the law." It is "guilty behavior and remorseful awareness of having done something wrong."

Were it not for the feeling of guilt, anarchy would

115

exist. Merited guilt serves some useful functions in our society. Unmerited guilt, which is imposed upon us by someone else for an imagined wrong, can be destructive and debilitating. Merited guilt is closely akin to empathy, which enables us to, in a real sense, feel the way the victim feels. As a result, we are more likely to deal more sensitively with that person in the future. If we, as wrongdoers, have no sense of remorse, chances are excellent that we will repeat the action and further damage the individual and destroy any possibility of a reconciliation or a permanent relationship.

Message: The next time you feel guilty about something, analyze it and if it is merited guilt, get excited—because that means you're on the way to being a better person. If it's unmerited guilt, simply reject it and go on with your life.

～

Overheard in a courtroom: Said the judge to the accused, "My inclination is to find you guilty, but hey, who am I to judge?"

Dress for Success

*If you don't feel good about yourself, you will have
a limited capacity to believe in others.*

One of the major problems in our society today is
the lack of pride many people have in their personal
appearance. Research clearly proves that a neat appearance and manner of dress has a direct bearing on conduct and performance. It is also instrumental in gaining
employment and has a bearing on your future with the
company that employs you. The person who hires you
forms an opinion of you in roughly three seconds, and
that opinion is a factor in every decision made about
you for several months. Unfortunately, a reasonably
high percentage of our population appear to deliberately dress to make themselves look unattractive and,
therefore, less desirable as employees, associates,
friends, or mates.

My friend and fellow training consultant, Nido
Qubein, in his *Executive Briefing* newsletter, says that
"pride is closely tied to self-esteem." He quotes Robert
W. Darvon, a founder of Scandinavian Design, Inc.,
who says, "There's only one thing that counts in a

business—building the self-esteem of your employees. Nothing else matters, because what they feel about themselves is what they give to your customers. If an employee comes to work not liking his job, not feeling good about himself, you can be sure that your customers will go away not liking or feeling good about your company."

The way you feel about your employees has an influence on the way they feel about themselves, which, in turn, has a direct bearing on their performance. You can make your people feel better about themselves by treating them with dignity and respect. The reality is that the way you treat your internal customers (your employees) is the way they will treat your external customers when they encounter them.

~

No matter how much money a woman has to spend, she can't dress in the latest styles unless she has the nerve.

Grow/Swell

Our ego is our silent partner—too often with a controlling interest.

As a rookie salesman I had a very difficult time getting started. However, once the ball started rolling, I enjoyed a spectacular four-year run of success. This led to a career change and new job in New York City. It was exciting and rewarding, but required that I leave home each morning before my two little girls were awake and most of the time when I returned at night they were already asleep. I could not handle that style of parenting, so in just three months' time we moved back to Columbia, South Carolina.

I got into a promotional-type business and temporarily enjoyed some success that quickly evaporated. At that point I stopped growing and started swelling, which led to sixteen additional job and career changes within the following five years. I became a super-critic, a know-it-all, and a very difficult person to work with. One of the companies I briefly worked for was an insurance company that had been in business for many years. This astonished me because they were obviously way behind the times and I had some absolutely brilliant ideas that would revolutionize their business and expand their market share. They rejected these very significant ideas. I left in a huff, wondering how they would ever survive—which, incidentally, they did.

After five frustrating years I finally had a reality check and realized that the success I enjoyed earlier had come because I had completely committed myself to improving what I did instead of assuming I knew it all. I made a strong commitment to the new company I represented and worked hard and enthusiastically, while continually acquiring new information from those who had beaten many a path before I came along. Interestingly enough, results were excellent and progress was steady so that just two years later I was back on a career path that has been most rewarding and satisfying.

I hope the message is clear. Keep growing. Don't start swelling.

≈

EGO stands for "Edging God Out."

Loving Your Child

If you will set the example, you don't need to set the rules.

As a young father, my mother frequently said to me, "Your children more attention pay to what you do than what you say." She also repeatedly said that if you "set the example, you won't need to make many rules." Later in life I heard someone else say that rules without a relationship lead to rebellion. I believe the statements my mother made, combined with the latter one, can lay the basis for a marvelous relationship and the raising of positive, morally sound, successful youngsters in our racist, sexist, and violent society of today.

My friend Jay Strack says that when you repeatedly express your acceptance of your child, you are giving that child the knowledge that you really do love him or her—and that's what gives them the all-important sense of security. He points out that when you express your appreciation for your child, you're giving him or her a feeling and sense of significance, which obviously is tremendously confidence-building. When your child sees that you pay attention to your mate and to your employer, as well as to adults of your acquaintance, they make the association that these other people are important, so when you make yourself available to your child for conversation and activities, that very availability gives your child a feeling of importance.

Dr. Strack also points out that when you demonstrate genuine parental affection on a regular basis with hugs, pats, and motherly or fatherly kisses, you're letting them know they are lovable.

To sum this up, when you give your child a feeling of security, significance and importance, and the knowledge that he or she is lovable, your child is going to be secure, confident, loving, and grateful. That's a pretty good start on life.

~

Everybody knows how to raise children, except the people who have them. (P. J. O'ROURKE)

I Believe in Braces

True grit is making a decision and standing by it, doing what must be done. No moral man can have peace of mind if he leaves undone what he knows he should have done.

—JOHN WHITE

Like most parents, my wife and I believe that straight teeth are a real asset to a person, so we invested in braces for three of our children who needed them. By spending a considerable sum of money for a beautiful smile, we believe we have received more than a good return on that investment. Our granddaughter, Katherine, got lovely results from wearing her braces. When I see an adult wearing braces and the opportunity presents itself, I commend him or her for their foresight and willingness to suffer some temporary pain and possible embarrassment in order to achieve a long-term benefit.

I say all of this to point out that a good smile is important, but at the same time I would like to emphasize that good character is substantially more important. I'm puzzled as to why we don't invest more of our resources in the teaching of character foundation to more of our children. Evidence is solid that the foundation stones of honesty, character, integrity, the right attitude, hard work, thrift, dependability, and a host of other qualities are the things that separate those people who really succeed in their professions and personal lives from those who enjoy only moderate success.

Our Founding Fathers were taught those foundational qualities from birth. Actually, over 90 percent of all the educational thrust in those days, according to the Thomas Jefferson Research Institute, was aimed at teaching ethical, moral, and spiritual values. Its effectiveness is evidenced by the lives of Washington, Adams, Madison, Monroe, Franklin, and numerous others. I believe if all of us would analyze this approach to life, we would get just as enthusiastic about character development as we are winning smiles. Straighten your teeth and you will have a winning smile. Straighten and strengthen your character and life will smile on you.

~

Talk is cheap until you hire a lawyer.

Economic Need and Crime

Character is not made in a crisis, it is only revealed.

For years I have heard on television and read in newspapers that a poor person who could not find a job was, if not expected to turn to crime, at least excused for doing so. Unfortunately, the more this idea is promoted, the more likely it is to occur, especially among those who do not have a strong character base. The facts concerning this issue are interesting, and as a friend of mine was inclined to say, "Everyone is entitled to his own opinion, but no one is entitled to the wrong facts."

I was raised during the Great Depression, so I was familiar with an occasional knock at the back door by someone asking for something to eat in exchange for some work they could do around the house or garden. Interestingly enough, virtually no one asked for free food—they wanted to work for it instead. Statistics clearly validate that the crime rate coming out of the depression was actually lower than it was when we entered the depression.

An article in the *Financial Post* by David Frum points out that the identical situation occurred in

Canada. He stated that statistics confirmed that in Canada there was "an overall five percent drop" in criminality between 1992 and 1993. This, despite the fact that 1993 should have seen an increase in crime. Instead, faced with plant closures, job losses, and shrinking social services, the Canadians became less inclined to break into houses and steal from the owners.

The reality is people do what they're taught and expected to do. If we will eliminate the concept that poverty breeds crime and more carefully teach that the right way is the best way, we will see further reductions in crime. In many cases an economic belt-tightening is a character-building experience that helps us learn to get along without many of the so-called "necessities of life," so we emerge from the economic challenges stronger and better prepared to build a more successful future.

~

About the only thing that can lay down on the job and produce results is a hen.

One Definition of *Wisdom*

The secret of happiness is to admire without desiring.
—F. H. BRADLEY

There are sources of happiness that are quite independent of money. A millionaire does not enjoy a book more than a poor man. Plain food tastes as good to a worker who has earned his dinner as do the choicest delicacies to the man whose appetite is jaded from an unnatural diet. The outdoors is as beautiful to a factory girl as to the wife of a factory owner, and the member of the sand lot ball team gets as much fun out of his sport as does a polo player.

A lot was said in just a few words, wasn't it? It's one more way of saying that things that really count are available to virtually all of us in this great land of ours. Most of it boils down to a matter of choice. The poor man can go to the library and have access to the greatest books of all time, written by men and women who really have "been there and done that," in the vernacular of the day. In this way we can enjoy vicariously the experiences, share the wisdom, enjoy the beauty, join in the laughter, and share all the emotional rewards that go with being well-read and creative. We can also sit in the quietness of our home or yard and reflect on life and the beauty of the sunset.

Will Rogers said that most of us can be about as happy as we make up our minds to be. Turning off the television and visiting with a neighbor over the fence or inviting them into our living room for a cup of coffee, a game of checkers or chess, or simply to pop some popcorn or grill a hot dog will help make that happiness a reality.

Do some of these things and you will be able to look back and say, "Yes, life has been good to me." Wisdom consists of using and enjoying the things around us and sharing with our friends.

~

Happiness has one great advantage over wealth. Friends don't try to borrow it.

Handling Disappointments

Don't let the mistakes and disappointments of the past direct and control your future.

Question: How would you feel if you lost an Olympic gold medal by two-thousandths of a second? You probably wonder, *How could they measure that closely?* Mathematically speaking, the distance you can swim in two-thousandths of a second is about the thickness of a coat of paint. To have worked years and years and to have been so close to the ultimate prize and yet miss it by that length of time in a 400-meter individual medley, must have been a difficult pill to swallow.

A fascinating article in the December 1995 issue of *Sky Magazine* tells what happened to American swimmer Tim McKee. The event took place in the 1972 Olympics in Munich when Olympic swimming timing had just "converted from stopwatches to the use of electronic touch pads." At that time stopwatches were "still sliced no finer than a hundredth of a second," but the just-installed electronic touch pads could measure the distance to thousandths of a second. McKee had tied for first place with Gunnar Larsson of Sweden to the hundredth of a second, according to the stopwatch, but lost by two-thousandths of a second, according to the electronic touch pad.

To make the matter even worse, at the meet in Los Angeles in 1984, gold medals were awarded to both swimmers who had tied to the hundredth of a second. I'm certain the disappointment was intense for Tim McKee, but in life we have many disappointments. Those who go on to greater things dwell on the disappointments briefly and then move on. I hope Tim realized that his entire life was still in front of him and whether he won or lost the gold medal he would always have his innate ability, drive, character, determination, love, commitment, responsibility, and all of the other things that help make him successful in life.

~

Life is like a game of tennis. He who serves best seldom loses.

This Is Important

We frequently hear people say, "I'm a self-made man." Thus far I've never heard one say, "I'm a self-made failure."

We do live in a hurry-hurry world, and despite all of the timesaving, laborsaving approaches and devices available to us today, despite all of the technology for streamlining, it seems that our wishes and desires require more additional time than the new technology and planning provide. What this really means is we need to prioritize what is important to "keep the main thing the main thing."

The most fascinating example of this is the story about author and diplomat Clare Booth Luce. Ms. Luce told of her visit with John F. Kennedy when he was in the White House. She was known for her forthrightness and straightforward manner. She said to Mr. Kennedy, "Mr. President, you must get the Soviets out of this hemisphere." They talked a few minutes, then the phone rang and the president went off. He came back rather excited and said, "I got my textile bill passed! Now, what were you saying, Clare?" To this Ms. Luce responded, "Mr. President, there are many great men remembered in our civilization. Of one man, they said He went to a cross and died so that all men's sins may be forgiven. Of another man, they said he went in search of a new route to an old world and founded a new world. Of another it is said that he took up arms against his mother country and with a motley army of rebels defeated the greatest military power on earth to found a new nation. And of another it is said that he had to hide in the dark of night as he came into Washington, and grieved for four years that the nation might be half-slave and half-free. Mr. President, of none of these great men was it said, 'He got his textile bill passed.'"

Our priorities are important and once we get them in order great things can happen in our lives.

~

He had his own train of thought and nobody else was on board.

Personality or Character?

Reputation is what folks think you are. Personality is what you seem to be. Character is what you really are.

John Maxwell, one of the top leadership authorities in America, says that most people would rather work on their personality than on their character, and how right he is. Perhaps that is because the personality development brings more immediate rewards, is less demanding and, in most cases, involves little sacrifice on our part. Personality development involves learning new conversational skills, style, or developing a speaking ability.

The development of character is more profound, is considerably more difficult, and often involves making changes that are at least temporarily uncomfortable and often very demanding. The changing of habits is always a difficult procedure. The development of virtues also requires time because it means we must discipline some of our appetites and passions. Keeping promises and being sensitive to the feelings and convictions of others are not things that most of us do naturally. We have to work at them. Character development is the best indication of maturity.

Yes, it is more difficult to develop character than personality and yes, it's true that the rewards are not as immediate. However, the long-term rewards are infinitely greater. To value oneself is important, but to be able at the same time to subordinate yourself to higher purposes and principles is the paradoxical essence of highest humanity and it is the foundation for effective leadership. I believe I'm safe in saying that in today's world, the need for character and leadership outweighs the need for more people with more personality. Fortunately, when you develop the character, the personality develops far more easily and more naturally.

~

Good times reveal part of your character, tough times reveal all of it.

Walking in Their Shoes

*The one absolutely unselfish friend that man can
have in this selfish world, the one that never deserts
him . . . is his dog.*

—GEORGE VEST

On the morning of November 20, my executive assistant, Laurie Magers, told me that she would probably not be in the next day because she had to take her mother's puppy, Muffin, to the veterinarian to be spayed. This will surprise many people who have known me for so many years, but just a few months ago I would have thought to myself, *I just don't understand somebody taking off to have something done to a dog.* I would be happy to take off work for my children and grandchildren, but pets were a different matter. My children always had pets because they loved them and I loved my children. But I could not understand how anyone could form such deep, emotional attachments to pets.

In March of 1995, however, things underwent a change when daughter Cindy talked my wife into attending a dog show with her. There she saw a little Welsh Corgi, a full-size dog with pint-size legs, which she immediately fell in love with. I'd always said never again would I have a pet, but my relationship with my wife is so important I "humored" her by agreeing that she could acquire one of those little dogs.

It took that little dog about three hours to worm his way into my heart. At the end of a week, ownership changed. He is now my dog, though my wife enjoys certain privileges like feeding and caring for him and playing with him when I'm gone. (Yes, that is my tongue you see in my cheek!)

When Laurie Magers told me she wanted to take care of her mother's little dog, I readily agreed. Funny, isn't it, how when we come to know the other person's feelings, it is so easy to understand those feelings. The message is clear: Don't be judgmental. Put yourself in the other person's position and try to think as they think or feel as they feel. I guarantee, you'll have more fun and much better relationships.

~

Bob Orben says that a typical American home is where you tell your dog to speak and your kids to shut up.

Handling Criticism

No one so thoroughly appreciates the value of constructive criticism as the one who's giving it.

The late comedian Groucho Marx said, "Whatever it is, I'm against it." My dictionary says that *criticism* is "the art of judging with propriety of the beauties and faults of a performance; remark on beauties and faults; critical observation, verbal or written."

Col. George Washington Goethals, the man who completed the Panama Canal, handled criticism effectively. During the construction he had numerous problems with the geography, climate, and mosquitoes. Like all mammoth projects, he had his critics back home who constantly harped on what he was doing and predicted that he would never complete the project. However, he stuck to the task and said nothing. One day an associate asked him, "Aren't you going to answer the critics?" "Yes," Goethals responded. "How" he was asked. "With the canal," Goethals replied. Though that approach didn't bring instant satisfaction, the canal itself brought long-term vindication.

Aristotle said criticism was meant as a standard of

judging will. Addison said it was ridiculous for any man to criticize the works of another if he has not distinguished himself by his own performance.

The world is hard on critics but on occasion they have real value. Ask yourself this question: *What interest does this person (critic) have in me?* A parent, teacher, employer, or coach has a vested interest in your performance. Unfortunately, many of them do not know how to effectively build up a person while giving suggestions that can make a difference. The key is to criticize the performance and not the performer. My mother once criticized my performance by saying, "For most boys this would be all right. But you're not most boys—you're my son and my son can do better than that." She had "criticized the performance," because it needed improvement, but she had praised the performer because he needed the praise.

~

Honest criticism is hard to take, particularly when it comes from a relative, a friend, an acquaintance, or a stranger. (FRANKLIN P. JONES)

Memory Is Important

Be like an eraser—recognize your mistakes, learn from your mistakes, and then erase them from your memory.

When someone wonders if I remember such and such an event or so-and-so, if the answer is no one of my favorite responses is to smile and acknowledge that no, I don't. Then I explain that I have a brilliant memory—it's just awfully short.

The truth is, memory is the key to many things. If we don't remember things, we are hopelessly lost and are placed in a confinement of sorts. However, there are some things you can do effective immediately that will improve your memory substantially. Douglas Hermann, Ph.D., in his book, *Super Memory,* points out that practice alone can improve "global" memory and substantially boost retrieval ability in certain areas of life. He says when you practice specific memory tasks, you can produce spectacular results.

Dr. Hermann says that most people who attempt to learn a long string of numbers read to them normally will remember about seven of the numbers correctly.

However, he says that after practicing for several months, many people can remember forty, fifty, sixty, or even as many as eighty numbers in a string. The only problem is that it does require some work and a commitment to the objective.

Dr. Hermann points out that most people normally can recall about a third of what they know. However, after a month of daily practicing to recall specific bits of information, they can dramatically improve, whether it's remembering a geographical location, a historical fact, or a personal event that took place many years earlier. This proves that if we do have a "poor memory," it's probably caused by an untrained or lazy memory. Work on that memory. You'll have more fun, be more effective, more productive, and happier in the process.

~

If you want to test your memory, try to remember what you were worrying about a year ago.

The Ten-Day Leap

We all find time to do what we really want to do.
—WILLIAM FEATHER

For most of us the arrival of a highly anticipated event—such as the birth of a new baby, a long-awaited vacation, the return home of a loved one, or the big game we've been looking forward to—seems to take forever.

On the other hand, if it's one of those dreaded events like April 15, the date a divorce becomes final, admission to the hospital for major surgery, or any event that brings pain, despair, or a sense of loss, the calendar rushes forward with breathtaking speed.

Regardless of whether you approach a particular date with anticipation or dread, you will be fascinated to know that on February 24, 1582, a church commission appointed by Pope Gregory XIII decided to change the calendar, dropping ten days and adopting a "leap year." For those countries that accepted the change, the date immediately became ten days later.

I have no information as to the resulting chaos and confusion that undoubtedly took place following the time/date change. I can imagine that the people who happened to have birthdays during those ten days were somewhat chagrined that they had missed out on a birthday or anniversary, which generally brings more pleasure than pain.

In this day of litigation, many employees would probably sue their employers if they were not paid for the ten days they didn't work. Some of the creditors would be besieged with threats and pleas if they were unwilling to bend the rules and give a few days of grace to people who were in debt to them.

Today, however, if we live our lives one day at a time, and if we do the best we can each day, we are making the best preparation for tomorrow. After all, today is the tomorrow of yesterday that we were going to do so much with. Do "so much" every day, and all your tomorrows will be better.

❧

Time flies. It's up to you to be the navigator. (ROBERT ORBEN)

Busy but Polite

The first responsibility of a leader is to define reality. The last is to say thank you. In between the two the leader must become a servant and a debtor. That sums up the progress of an artful leader.

—MAX DEPREE

Theodore Roosevelt, former president of the United States, has been described as founder of the Bull Moose Party, the man who led his troops up San Juan Hill in the Spanish-American War, a big-game hunter, family man, civic servant, and a host of other things.

His life story would indicate that he was not only an extraordinarily successful man, but surely one of the busiest and best-organized ever. However, with all of his "busy-ness," even during his campaign trips, when the demands on his time were the greatest, he still retained some of those human qualities that made him so successful. Simple example: He never forgot to thank others who did things for him. On his whistle-stop tours during his campaign trips, he always left his private car to stop and thank the engineer and fireman for a safe and comfortable trip. True, it took only a few minutes of his time, but when your minutes are so few, they are quite important. However, he felt that those minutes were well invested and he enjoyed meeting the people who had served him so well. In the process he made friends for life. Doing simple little things, thinking of the other person, endeared him to people all across America, which certainly was a significant reward for the few minutes it took him to say thank you.

Someone once said that you could always tell a "big man" by the way he treated a "little" man. By that yardstick alone you would have to agree that Theodore Roosevelt was a "big" man. Message: Take time to be kind and to say "thank you." The returns can be great.

~

Two ways to make every day a better day: Think and thank.

Class

Some people leave their footprints in the sands of time, but others leave only the mark of a heel.

From time to time someone gives another individual the ultimate compliment when he or she says, "You are a 'class act,'" or they simply describe a specific behavior and say, "That's class." Occasionally a master of ceremonies will introduce an individual by saying, "If you go to the dictionary and look up the word *class,* you will see a picture of your speaker this evening."

A person with class is an individual of integrity, someone you would love to have as a parent or child, a friend or a neighbor, a mentor or an adviser. In short, class identifies a person who is "top drawer," one who goes the extra mile by being gracious to everyone who courteously serves them.

I love the description given in comments made by Bill Daniels, who said that "class is something you choose for yourself. It's competing honestly, confronting problems head-on, taking accolades with grace and humility and not knocking your competitors. If you have class you're loyal to both yourself and to those around you. Class is born out of self-respect and a healthy respect for others. Everything in this world is not always attainable. Fortunately, class is."

Class is the coach who gives every child on the team his turn "at bat" without regard to the youngster's ability or the won-lost record of the team.

I encourage you to identify someone who is a class act and use that person as a role model. The individual might not be rich and famous or even brilliant, but a person of class is one we can all aspire to be.

Narrow-minded people are similar to narrow-necked bottles. The less they have in them, the more noise they make pouring it out. (ALEXANDER POPE)

She's Tough—But Loving

Just about anyone can make a living. The duty and opportunity of everyone is to make a life.

Sister Connie Driscoll is a nun who is working miracles among the drug- and alcohol-addicted homeless in Chicago. Her program keeps 95 percent of her formerly homeless clients from ever returning to the streets. Her cost is about $7.35 per person per day.

How? She starts with a 7:30 P.M. curfew and a 6:30 A.M. wake-up call. She also includes periodic shakedowns and drug tests. She holds each of the residents accountable for their own behavior and performance. Her facility is St. Martin de Poores House of Hope, where "tough love" really does mean tough.

Sister Connie is a Korean War veteran who grew up on a farm where she was no stranger to manual labor. Sledgehammers in hand, she and colleague Sister Therese smashed through a few brick walls in their decrepit, donated building, which they soon filled with homeless women and children. Some of her tenants complained about the food and others refused to make their beds or used drugs on the premises. They even said, "I don't have to sweep the floor, because I have the right." At this point, Sister Connie simply said, "Nope." She began searching under toilet seats and lifting mattresses, looking for drugs. She called in a police SWAT team for a 7:00 A.M. drug raid on her residence. She means business. Residents subject themselves to this treatment because they know that it is their last hope to escape the misery that has become a part of their lives.

Twelve-step Narcotics Anonymous and Alcoholics Anonymous sessions are mandatory, as are high school equivalency classes and sessions in child care, housekeeping, and preparing for job interviews. Staff members teach the women comparison shopping and checkbook balancing. Sister Connie knows that for most of her clients the chief problem is not lack of money, but lack of personal responsibility. She tells the women, "No matter who caused your problems, only you can solve them." Wouldn't it be neat if we had a Sister Connie, with her staff of committed people who work for virtually nothing and give it their all, in places all over the country?

~

Think about it. The people who make mistakes are the ones who make everything else. Those who make no mistakes make nothing else.

Challenge or Paralysis?

Sometimes it's not easy to apologize, to begin over, to admit error, to take advice, to be unselfish, to keep on trying, to be honest, to profit by mistakes, to forgive and forget, to think and then to act, to shoulder a deserved blame—but it always pays.

Dwayne Pingston is paralyzed from the waist down—but not immobilized anywhere. In 1983, when he was only nineteen years old, he avoided a head-on collision by swerving sharply to his right. In the process he hit the shoulder of the road and was thrown from the car. His neck snapped and his legs were rendered useless.

For many that would have meant the end of hopes, dreams, activity, and ambition, but for Dwayne it simply was a challenge to take what he had left and use it to maximum ability. He has an incredible attitude. He is good-natured and unassuming and is more active than most people with two strong legs. He's an enthusiastic fisherman and deer hunter. He plays wheelchair basketball for the Easter Seals All-American Team and helped start a basketball camp for thirty inner-city kids with disabilities ranging from cerebral palsy to spina bifida. He races cars at the Milan Dragway near Ann Arbor, Michigan, swims exuberantly, and has helped crew a thirty-eight-foot sailboat in the Port Huron to Mackinac race.

In his spare time he restores old cars and also works for a living, holding down two jobs. He delivers custom-designed cars from Jaguar of Troy to customers across the country. His sense of humor is incredible and he even points out advantages in having no feeling in his legs, as when he broke both ankles playing wheelchair rugby.

Does this mean that he is in denial? No. It simply means he has recognized the fact that he is paralyzed from the waist down and will be that way for life. He can either bemoan his fate or recognize all of the things he still can do and proceed to do them. There's a tremendous lesson here for all of us: Don't moan about what we might have lost; rejoice about what we still have.

~

Conscience is what hurts when everything else feels so good.

Hope—The First Step
Toward Success

No one demands a lot of explanation for any job done right.

Possibly the oldest motivational sales story in existence is the one about the salesperson who went to Africa to sell shoes and reported back to his company that it was impossible to sell shoes there because nobody wore them. His replacement reported back that it was the most exciting market he had ever seen because nobody had shoes. One salesperson had hope—the other had no hope, and without hope, there will be no effort.

Several years ago when unemployment was high I met a lady whose close friend had been unemployed for a year and had given up hope. That's fairly easy to understand, but financial needs continue, regardless of the status of our hope. I asked the lady to share with her friend some statistical data that would be helpful. I pointed out that roughly 140 million Americans had jobs and that 22 percent of them, or roughly 30 million people, were working on jobs they did not have the previous year. That means 30 million people had been "hired" in the past twelve months, so approximately 2.5 million people had gotten new jobs each month for the past year, more than 600,000 had gotten new jobs each week, and more than 120,000 people were hired each working day. I encouraged her to share with her friend that since 120,000 jobs would be filled each day, he should go out with a prepared résumé and an optimistic, upbeat approach to life, fully armed with references and determination, and find just one of those jobs.

I'm convinced that if her friend followed that advice, he got one of those jobs. The key difference is the word *attitude,* and, according to studies conducted at both Harvard and Stanford, 85 percent of the reason people get jobs and get ahead in those jobs is because they have the right mental attitude. That approach will convert the unemployed to the employed.

∼

Virtually no one who loses his job says, "I got me fired."

Necessity—The Mother of Invention

Life is like an ice-cream cone—just when you think you've got it licked, it drips all over you.

From childhood, ice cream has been my favorite dessert. Coming from a large family and raised during the depression, we had an occasional "churn" of ice cream on Sunday afternoon. We didn't get much at a serving, so that made it particularly enjoyable. Over the years my passion for ice cream did nothing but grow and at one time I could quickly rattle off the four best ice creams available in America and, interestingly enough, the best flavors came from four different companies. To this day I find it difficult to pass the ice cream store without a quick stop for at least a single-, if not a double-dip. Unfortunately, my body retains ice cream, so I seriously limit my intake today.

This leads me to a fascinating little story on ice cream and the ice-cream sundae. A merchant from Wisconsin named Smithson, out of necessity, invented the ice-cream sundae in 1890. They did not deliver on Sunday in those days, so to avoid running short he reduced the amount of ice cream with each order and added chocolate syrup or some special fruit topping to the mixture. The mixture was so well received that he was asked by his customers to serve it on the other days of the week as well. He wanted to meet his customers' needs and desires, but some people objected to the use of the word *Sunday* because it was the Lord's Day. They felt that to call an ice cream dish after the Lord's Day was profane. That's when he modified the spelling to "sundae." Today the ice-cream sundae is still a favorite among millions of people.

Just think—we never would have had the sundae had there not been a shortage of ice cream. The next time you run short of something, think of how you can stretch it out. Who knows? Maybe it will be a bonanza like the sundae.

～

I like chocolate ice cream, but when I go fishing I use worms because the fish like worms.

The Hawk and the Sparrow

The instant you set a goal a light goes on in your future.

—JIM PALUCH

This morning I spotted a large hawk in the willow tree behind my home. There were two or three small birds, which I believe were sparrows, driving that hawk nuts! He would get comfortably situated and one of them would dive at him, quickly followed by another. The hawk moved three or four times, but those little birds continued to harass him until he took off for parts unknown. As I watched this little drama, I was reminded of the difference between the hawk and the eagle. When the eagle is chased by his enemies, instead of ignoring them or trying to avoid them, he flies straight toward the sun. He has special coverings on his eyes that enable him to look directly at the sun one moment and in the next instant drop his eyes and spot a field mouse far below. He is safe when he heads for the light.

We can relate this example to men and women. Little people—and I do not refer to size—are easily harassed by small incidents in life, bugged by every criticism, and angered at barbs from others. They squirm and become defensive, but this only encourages the barb-throwers to keep after them. Men and women of integrity, however, who are confident within themselves, are not affected by what the "little" people say about them. Like the eagle, they hide from their enemies in the light because they know who they are and what they stand for. They understand that with integrity they have nothing to fear because they have nothing to hide.

Hopefully, the parallel is clear and there's a lesson there we can learn. Live with integrity, hide in the light.

~

If you're in debt, cheer up and sing. Remember that the birds have bills and that's what they do.

What Do You Expect?

You get better results if you have high expectations. This is true in science, math, reading, football, or band.

—CHARLES ADAIR

Speaker/author Mamie McCullough tells this story. Several years ago as she started the school year, second-grade teacher Frances Hurst of Rayville Parish, Rayville, Louisiana, was told that she had the "middle" class of students. At that time, all the students were grouped as either "low," "middle," or "high." This grouping or grading bothered Ms. Hurst quite a bit because she had never taught "ability grouping" before.

On her first day of class, the students told her they were the "middle group," and at that point Ms. Hurst went into action. She closed the door, placed paper over the glass in the windows, and told the students there had been a mistake and that they were actually the "high" group. From that point on, she treated them as though they were the high group. Her expectations for them were high; their own expectations and confidence grew, and at the end of the school year the SRA test (which is given to measure the achievement for each group) revealed that her group had tested one year ahead of the "high" group. Since this test was a class average, that meant that some of the students were testing much higher than the "high" group.

Someone once said that if you treat a person as he is you make him worse than he was, but if you treat that person as the individual he's capable of becoming you make him the best person possible. That's a marvelous philosophy because it's true. This was aptly proved by Ms. Frances Hurst. Wouldn't it be wonderful if every parent, teacher, and employer in America would treat everybody as if they were in the "high group"? Odds are dramatic that everything would be better. You can't influence everybody, but you can influence those you work and live with. Put them all in the high group— they'll climb higher and so will you.

~

If you go against the grain of the universe, you get splinters.

The Greats Didn't
Start That Way

Some great people make other people feel small, but really great people make everyone feel great.

Basketball fans who watch the Chicago Bulls in action today, if they don't know the story, would probably be astonished to learn that Michael Jordan, considered by many to be the greatest basketball player who ever lived, was cut from the squad when he was a sophomore in high school. Fortunately, he didn't quit playing and the results speak for themselves.

Football fans who have followed the NFL for many years consider Joe Namath to be one of the finest athletes, and certainly one of the smartest, most confident quarterbacks with a great arm who ever played the game. As a sophomore in high school he weighed 135 pounds and was five feet seven. He came from an athletic family, had athletic abilities, and although his older brothers were helpful, he was the fourth-string quarterback on the JV squad. After the second game he approached Bill Ross, the athletic director and head coach at Beaver Falls High School, saying he was thinking about quitting the game "because I'm too small to ever be a quarterback."

Bill Ross smiled and agreed that Joe was too small then and that he wouldn't play much as a sophomore, but "I knew he was a good athlete and that he would grow. I told Joe that it was the wrong time to quit, that he hadn't proved himself one way or the other so I said, 'Go home and think about it overnight before you make your final decision.' The next afternoon he was back at practice. Before the end of the season the JV squad played Elwood City in an away game, Namath was phenomenal, and the football legend was on his way." Message: Don't quit.

∾

There are no victories at bargain prices.

A Timeless Truth

It's one of the most beautiful compensations of this life that no man can sincerely try to help another without helping himself.

—RALPH WALDO EMERSON

While going through my files I came across a blurb from *Catholic Digest* written by Mary Kinsolving, which is as relevant today as it was many years ago when it was written. Ms. Kinsolving tells a story of living in Manhattan where, as a child, her mother walked her to school four blocks away every morning and then walked home with her again in the afternoon. One hard winter her mother came down with pneumonia and Mary had to go to school and return home by herself. She states that on the way home the second day she fell on some ice while crossing the street and at that moment a car skidded toward her and came within inches of her before it stopped. "The driver helped me up," she said, "and I managed to get home but didn't tell my mother because I didn't want her to worry."

The next morning the streets were even icier and when she came to her first cross street she was terrified and stated that she stood at the intersection for a long time. Finally, an elderly woman came over to her and said, "I don't see very well. May I hold your hand when I cross the street?" She replied, "Oh, yes," and the elderly lady took her hand and "before long we were on the other side." Then Mary Kinsolving walked a short distance and looked back to see how the woman was doing. To her surprise, "She was crossing the street we had just crossed together and was walking by herself much faster than we had before." Ms. Kinsolving then realized that the lady had pretended poor eyesight only to help her cross the street. Much later in life she understood that she could overcome her own fears by helping someone else.

What marvelous advice from years gone past!

~

It's hard to tell what brings happiness—poverty and wealth have both failed.

You've Failed—Now Sit Down

One of the ironies of life is that at the very moment we're teaching our children to walk we must also be teaching them to walk away; that while we nourish the roots we must also help them spread their wings.
—EXECUTIVE SPEECHWRITER NEWSLETTER

Most parents experience the joy of watching their children turn over, then crawl, then stand up, and then take those first steps. With outstretched arms they stand two or three steps away and encourage the little one to come to them. Chances are about three trillion to one that when the baby falls down the parent is not going to say, "Okay, you had your chance—you blew it! So don't you ever try to walk again!" That's absurd, but isn't it equally absurd to think we can accomplish major things in our lives without experiencing reversals of some kind? We all need to remember that failure is an event, not a person, that success is a process and not just an instant happening. Few succeed overnight. Instead, they succeed over time.

Troy Aikman, Steve Young, Brett Favre, and Dan Marino are all extremely effective NFL quarterbacks and yet each of the four has thrown more incomplete passes than 99 percent of all the quarterbacks who ever threw a football. Obviously, along the way they also threw an awful lot of completions. The top salesperson in the organization probably missed more sales than 90 percent of the salespeople on the team, but they also made more calls than the others made. There's never been a doctor who served many patients who, despite his or her best efforts, did not lose some of them to death. But they understood that was part of life itself.

All of us need to remember there is a vast difference between failing in an event and failing in life. Once we understand that, our chances for success substantially increase. We need to remember that winners are people who got up one more time than they were knocked down.

~

Failure is the path of least persistence.

We Are Emotional

*How much more grievous are the consequences of
anger than the causes of it?*

—MARCUS AURELIUS

Most people pride themselves on making logical decisions, but research conclusively proves that we mainly make emotional decisions because we, at heart, are emotional beings. Question: Did you see the movie *E.T.*? If you answered yes, the next question is, Did you cry? Chances are about four thousand to one that you answered either "yes," or "almost." Now, is that logical? *E.T.* was the figment of a very fertile imagination and was neither human nor animal—and yet, your emotions were triggered and you shed tears as a result of the story.

Many of us reacted emotionally when our state passed mandatory seat belt laws. We griped, fussed, and complained, "What will the government be telling us to do next?" Strangely enough, no one complains about having to fasten a seat belt in an airplane. The reality is that a seat belt in a car dramatically reduces injury and possible death. However, when an airplane falls out of the sky a seat belt is seldom of any value.

Our emotions are important and when they're out of control it's not healthy. A *Psychology Today* article pointed out that if we were to think for just five minutes about some emotional event that made us angry and then think for a few minutes about something that enabled us to feel and accept appreciation, caring, and compassion, there would be a dramatic difference in our body's response. When we're angry our heart beats faster and we feel stress. "It's like driving your car with one foot on the brake and one foot on the accelerator. It costs a lot in gas and wear and tear on brakes and drivetrain," observes Rollin McCraty. However, when we think pleasant thoughts and feelings, the heart slows down, our system functions better, and our heart ends up in better shape.

Message: Train yourself to control your anger and instead think pleasant thoughts, remembering pleasant experiences, and you can divert anger into a healthy response.

∿

If you are patient in one moment of anger, you will escape a hundred days of sorrow.

Treat People Like Cows

Some regard private enterprise as if it were a preda-
tory tiger to be shot. Others look upon it as a cow
that they can milk. Only a handful see it for what it
really is—the strong horse that pulls the whole cart.
—WINSTON CHURCHILL

My dad died during the Great Depression when I
was five. Six of us children were too young to work outside the home, but all of us did our part around the
house. Our economic survival was built around five
milk cows and a large garden. We sold the surplus milk
and butter as well as many of the vegetables.

I was milking cows by the time I was eight years old
and I can tell you from experience that cows don't "give"
milk—you have to fight for every drop! I can also tell you
that the way you treat the cow has a direct bearing on the
quantity and the quality of the milk she produces. If you
beat her and treat her badly as you are preparing to milk
her, two things will happen. She will give less milk and
the milk might not be usable, because when she is angry
and upset the milk she produces is often bitter and useless. In addition, she might retaliate and kick you.

I'm not suggesting that you need to "kiss" the cow, but I am encouraging you to speak kindly to her and stroke her a time or two to let her know you appreciate her efforts. My mother loved her cows and expected her children to love them, too. As a result, we got maximum production from our cows, which gave us an extra bonus. After keeping one for two or three years, we raised her milk production so much Mom could sell that cow for considerably more money than she paid for her. For us that was a big plus.

Here's the message. Treat people kindly, gently, and with respect and consideration. They will respond favorably, and if they happen to be on your payroll they will work harder and be more productive. On the other hand, if you abuse them, they will be unable to do their best.

~

Laughter is the lotion for the sunburns of life.

168

Give What You've Got

There's only one way to succeed in anything and that is to give everything.

—VINCE LOMBARDI

Agnes W. Thomas tells the story of what happened when her next-door neighbor died and left a fourteen-year-old daughter named Amy who was often alone when her father was at work. "Amy spent much of her after-school time in my apartment, so I decided to teach her how to crochet.

"Over the years we spent many happy hours together as we worked. One Christmas we called a local nursing home and asked if they had any residents who would not be receiving gifts at Christmas. Amy and I took our crocheted lap robes to these people on Christmas Eve.

"The following year Amy married and moved away and later when she came back to our area with her beautiful, red-haired baby girl, she called and asked if I planned to visit the nursing home on Christmas Eve. 'I want to be with you,' she said, 'but I haven't had any time to crochet since Jennifer was born, so I don't have any gifts to take them.' 'That's all right,' I said, 'you can help me take mine.' 'No, I have a better idea,' she said, 'I'll take my greatest treasure—my baby.'

"Great merriment appeared on the faces of the elderly people when we walked into the room with that beautiful baby. 'Oh, she looks just like my daughter did when she was a baby,' exclaimed one of the residents. 'May I hold her?' asked another. Jennifer was passed around like a doll. That baby brought more joy and laughter than all of my crocheted lap robes. Amy was happy, too. 'They really liked my baby, didn't they?' she asked as we left the building. 'To make people happy, I guess you just give what you have.'"

How true. The human spirit is encouraged by the love and concern of another person, and what could be more encouraging and delightful to the elderly than holding an innocent baby? That's a real gift any time of the year.

~

You may give out, but never give up.

Workaholics or Peak Performers?

A person lost in his work has probably found his future.

In this day of corporate downsizing there is much fear in the marketplace. However, to a degree, there has always been a certain amount of fear as far as our employment security is concerned, and for a number of years the term *workaholic* has been a common one. I would like to point out, however, there is a difference between the "peak performer" and the "workaholic," and in the motives from which they work.

The workaholic frequently works out of fear and/or greed, either of which is a negative emotion that ultimately will lead to some serious problems in the individual's life. Excessive fear is never a healthy companion, and if the worker is getting to work early and staying extremely late because he or she fears losing their job, that's not healthy.

An even more destructive fear is the fear of dealing with difficulties at home. Many workaholics enjoy and are good at their jobs but they are unwilling to take the time necessary to communicate with a rebellious teenager or their mate. This factor keeps them on the job long hours and helps them avoid those confrontations. "Things" motivation also drives the workaholic. They want a newer, bigger house, a fancier car, or to be able to take longer, more exotic vacations. They're working to acquire things beyond their needs and often sacrifice their health and their families on the altar of work.

Peak performers work hard because they love what they're doing. They work smarter, love their jobs and the goods or services their jobs provide. They also love to provide adequately for their families. Evidence is irrefutable that loving what you do and the people you are doing it for is healthier, more productive, and even more financially rewarding than working out of fear or greed. Explore your motives. Working out of fear and/or greed can be emotionally and physically damaging. Working extra hours invested because of love is healthy up to a point.

Work for love.

~

When I was young I observed that nine out of every ten things I did were failures, so I did ten times more work.
(GEORGE BERNARD SHAW)

School vs. Finishing Education

Those who have not distinguished themselves at school need not on that account be discouraged. The greatest minds do not necessarily ripen the quickest.

—JOHN LUBBOCK

There's an old saying that you can finish school and even make it easy. That simply is not true of education. You never finish and it is seldom easy, but it's always important.

Myrtle Estella Shannon did both—acquired an education and finished school. It's true that she was ninety-one before she finished college, and seven decades had passed since she was a teenager, but Ms. Shannon received her bachelor of arts degree on Sunday, January 21, 1996. She is still spry with a great sense of humor and a large amount of enthusiasm.

Hers is an inspiring story of an African-American woman, raised in Vicksburg, Mississippi, at a time when members of her race were denied educational, social, and business opportunities. Her family eventually moved to Gary, Indiana, and still later to Chicago.

She finished high school at sixteen, went on to

business trade school when she was twenty, and earned a certificate in liberal arts from an adult education program at the University of Chicago when she was forty-seven. She started part-time at Roosevelt University in 1984 but had to stop in 1992 for cataract surgery. She returned to Roosevelt in 1995 to complete her final class for a degree.

Ms. Shannon always sat up front so she could be in the midst of intellectual discussions and because she could see and hear better. She was an above-average student, took some difficult courses and did well in them. During the years when she was not in school, she traveled abroad and collected mementos to remind her of a fulfilled life.

It's hard to understand how Ms. Shannon was able to persist for so many years when she had many opportunities to decide that it really wasn't worth the effort. But aren't we glad she finished and isn't she a marvelous example for all of us to follow?

~

Every time you graduate from the school of experience, somebody thinks up a new course.

Keep Your Finger in the Pie

Leadership implies movement toward something and convictions provide that direction.

—DON SHULA

Former Secretary of Education William J. Bennett, one of the guiding lights in the struggle to restore moral and ethical values in our society, tells this fascinating personal story. In the late spring of 1985 his wife, Elayne, who is a former teacher, urged him to visit schools and teach classes. "While we were still courting, she had seen me teach high school classes in Portland, Maine. Later, when I became education secretary, she told me, 'You're a good teacher and people will take you more seriously if they see you doing what you're talking about. In addition to talking about education, why don't you go out and show people you can teach somebody something?'" Bennett resisted and said, "I don't do retail now, I do wholesale." At that point Elayne persisted and said, "If you do some retail you'll do better wholesale." Good thinking.

What she was saying is as old as time itself. She was saying that by example he would be demonstrating the importance of and giving dignity to the teachers and the profession of teaching. Elayne was also saying that the real heroes of life are "down in the trenches," doing the job and encouraging others to do the same.

That thought carries a message for every business executive. If executives are knowledgeable about every phase of their business, they will have a greater appreciation for what the rest of their staff is doing. Obviously, the CEO of a Fortune 500 company, or even a moderately sized company, cannot know everything about every operation. However, they should regularly explore what happens in each department and talk with the people doing the jobs. Not only will this interest bring them closer to their people, but the knowledge they will acquire will help them to more effectively lead the company.

~

Don't expect your "leader-ship" to come in if you're unwilling to unload the cargo.

The Responsibility Is Yours

You are the only person who can use your ability. That is an awesome responsibility because as a steward of your talent and ability, you have no options. You have been entrusted with something that you alone can develop and use.

Abraham Lincoln said, "You cannot escape the responsibility of tomorrow by evading it today."

The "blame game" goes back to the beginning. God told Adam and Eve when He placed them in the Garden that they could have it all, except they were not to eat the fruit of the tree in the middle of the Garden.

However, they ate the fruit of that tree and in the evening, as God walked in the Garden, He called for Adam and Adam responded, "Over here, Lord." Then God asked the question, "Adam, did you eat the fruit of the tree in the middle of the Garden?" God already knew the answer but He wanted Adam to respond. Adam, however, did the "manly thing" and replied, "Lord, let me tell You about that woman You gave me!" and that's where the ball started its long, unending roll. God then asked Eve if she had eaten the fruit, and Eve passed the ball along and said, "Lord, let me tell You about that snake!" And, of course, the snake didn't have a leg to stand on!

Theologically speaking, I know I'm in error when I make that statement. However, I am not in error when I say each one of us must recognize that it is not "his fault, her fault, or their fault"—it is our responsibility.

To solve the problem, we need to go back to the beginning and, starting in the family, teach our children responsibility. Next, we should pass the baton to the teachers in the schools and insist they continue to teach responsible behavior. Then when our young people have learned their lessons well, they will practice responsibility in their personal lives and the workplace as well. When this happens, the responsibility crisis will end and we'll have a better society as a result.

~

The price of greatness is responsibility.

Those Famous Sayings

Thus far, psychologists haven't explained why unlikely gossip becomes plausible when heard in a whisper.

—GEORGE GREGORY

In our country we have a number of proverbs or wise sayings that have been handed down from generation to generation. For example, "A stitch in time saves nine," "A watched pot never boils," and "Saved by the bell," to name just a few.

Many of these sayings have fascinating origins and when we explore those origins we not only learn a bit of history, but some practical philosophy and lessons also come from them. One of my favorites is "Saved by the bell." This goes back in history to 1696 when a sentry by the name of John Hatfield was on duty at Windsor Castle in England. Sentry duty was taken seriously in those days and it basically meant staying alert. However, Hatfield was accused of sleeping at his post and neglecting that duty. He was given a trial at which he spoke in his own defense. He claimed that he had not been sleeping and had, in fact, heard the bell of St. Paul's

Cathedral twenty miles away in London strike thirteen times. This was an unbelievable claim, which he made in his own defense, and Hatfield was found guilty. In that day and time, sentries found guilty of dereliction of duty were sentenced to death on the gallows.

A kind or curious—or perhaps both—person thought enough of the unusual nature of Hatfield's story to make some inquiries about his unusual defense. This individual discovered that, indeed, the bell at St. Paul's had struck thirteen times. There were others in the community who had also heard and counted those thirteen strikes. Hatfield received a reprieve and lived to the ripe old age of 102. He was, literally, "saved by the bell" (from *Capper's Weekly*).

Message: We should be careful about how we convict other people until all the evidence is in. Common sense and fair play demand nothing less.

❧

Wives often laugh at their husbands' jokes not because the jokes are clever, but because the wives are.

That Is Most Unfortunate

An apology is sensitivity and courtesy too late.

A few years ago a unique service was started in Fort Worth, Texas, entitled "An Apology Service." The founder and creator of the service was Ms. Kathy Warman. For just $6, Ms. Warman would pick up the phone and with her Southern charm and accent, offer an apology to the person you might have offended.

Unfortunately, there is no question that such a service is needed, but isn't it tragic that there is a need to have someone else apologize for you? Whatever happened to personal responsibility? It is inconceivable that anyone would be unwilling or unable to call and apologize for having offended a client, customer, friend, or relative. And regardless of how effective Ms. Warman might have been, there is a major difference between doing it yourself and hiring someone else to do it for you.

In most cases, the offended person is partially placated by the professional apologizer, but surely he or she would wonder why the offender didn't pick up the telephone and offer the apology personally. First, an apology is almost always accepted. Second, it indicates that you are now thinking straight, recognize your mistake, and want to rectify it and put the relationship on a more friendly basis. Third, and perhaps most important, the benefit you receive from apologizing personally is dramatically increased. It means you have accepted your responsibility, faced up to a difficult assignment, gone through the process, survived, and even thrived as a result. Difficult? Yes, but a tremendous learning and growth experience.

Historically speaking, those who do the difficult things end up doing the easy things more effectively. Remember, an apology is often politeness too late. So, think about it. The next time you've offended someone and need to apologize, do it yourself. You will have more and better friends, more and better clients and customers, and a better self-image as a result.

∼

You know it's time to lose weight when your mate tells you to "pull in your stomach" and you already have.

Laughter Is Good Medicine

Laughter is the hand of God on the shoulder of a troubled world.

There's nothing new about the observation that laughter is good medicine. It goes back hundreds, even thousands of years when the court jester had the task of entertaining royalty and the heads of state. If he was good at his job and performed well, his rewards would be considerable, and if he put on a lousy performance there was a reasonably good chance that he would lose his head—I mean *really* lose his head! Over a period of time, however, these court jesters learned that being humorous did much more than just entertain.

Pat Willhoit, otherwise known as Dr. Isaac the Clown, points out that laughter is one of the greatest mental tonics known to man and is the second most powerful human emotion an individual can express. The first, incidentally, is love. He says, "You can't laugh and be mad, you can't laugh and worry, because stress, worry, and laughter are not compatible. Laughter is low-calorie, caffeine-free, no sodium, no preservatives or additives; it's one hundred percent natural and one size fits all. Laughter truly is God's gift. You can get high on laughter but never 'O.D.' Laughter is contagious; once it starts, little can be done to stop it. Laughter never felt bad, committed a crime, started a war, or broke up a relationship. Laughter is shared by the giver and the receiver. Laughter costs nothing and is not taxable."

It sounds as if laughter could well be the cure for many of life's ills, so laugh a lot and you'll live a lot.

~

Laughter is the jam on the toast of life. It adds flavor, keeps it from being too dry, and makes it easier to swallow. (DIANE JOHNSON)

Leave Something Behind

Mountaintops inspire leaders but valleys mature them.

—F. PHILIP EVERSON

Each of us has been left a lot by preceding generations. Dr. Thomas Gibbs Jr. says, "Every man has leaned upon the past. Every liberty we enjoy has been bought at incredible cost. There is not a privilege nor an opportunity that is not the product of other men's labors. We drink every day from wells we have not dug; we warm ourselves by fires we have not kindled; we live by liberties we have not won; we are protected by institutions we have not set up. No man lives unto himself alone. All the past is invested in him. A new day is a good time to say, 'I am under obligation to accept my share of the world's grief, my share of its opportunities.'"

Life is a lot like tennis—he who serves best seldom loses. Responsibility demands that we pay our own way and leave something behind for those who will follow. Leaving a heritage of having lived an ethical, moral, and productive life is something all of us can do. Teaching a functional illiterate how to read would enrich that person's life and enable him or her to make a bigger and better contribution to society. Acts such as giving a word of encouragement and setting an example of gentle kindness and thoughtful consideration for others are much-needed in our society today and would leave your impact on future generations.

Unfortunately, too many of us labor under the illusion that unless we can do something monumental, there is nothing we can do. That's too bad, because doing something for others brings greater happiness to oneself.

~

Parents: Train up a child in the way he should go, and go there yourself once in a while.

Careful What You Leave

The measure of a life, after all, is not its duration but its donation.

—CORRIE TEN BOOM

I love the story told by Glenn Van Ekeren in his *Speaker's Sourcebook*. It was a hot, humid day in the middle of Kansas City. The eight-hour shift seemed especially long for the veteran bus driver. Suddenly, a young woman, apparently upset about something, let loose with a string of unforgettable, not to mention unrepeatable, words. The bus driver, looking in his overhead mirror, could sense everyone around her was embarrassed by the string of profanity. Still mumbling, the angry passenger began to disembark a few blocks later. As she stepped down, the bus driver calmly said, "Madam, I believe you're leaving something behind." She quickly turned and snapped, "Oh? And what is that?" "A very bad impression," the bus driver responded.

It has been generally recognized as truth that our first impression of a person is one we will hold for the longest time, and the last impression we have of that person is held almost as long. Political consultant Roger Ailes has said that we generally make up our mind within a matter of seconds of meeting a person as to whether or not we're going to like them or even trust them. Those few seconds are important and will affect our decisions regarding that person for a long time.

One of the best ways to make a good first impression is with a smile and a pleasant demeanor. Yes, the first and last impressions are important, but over the long haul it's trust and character that determine the length and extent of most relationships. Think about it. Make good first impressions, make good last impressions, and in between be the right kind of person. You'll collect an awful lot of friends and admirers.

~

Waiter to customer: "What do you mean the service is poor? I haven't given you any yet."

Teamwork Is Important

Nobody made a greater mistake than he or she who did nothing because one could do only a little.

In the days of yesteryear most organs were in churches and had to be "pumped" by someone behind the scenes. Once a talented soloist was giving a concert in a church and was extraordinarily well received. During intermission the singer-organist walked backstage where he was greeted by a pleasant, cheerful gentleman who was pumping the organ. He acknowledged the singer, saying, "We're putting on quite a performance, aren't we?" The singer responded, "What do you mean, 'we'?" and turned and walked back onstage. As he started to play, with a flourish he hit the keys of the organ and there was nothing—not a sound came forth. He quickly went backstage and said to the gentleman pumping the organ, "Yes, *we* really are giving a performance, aren't we?"

Most people who are behind the scenes do not receive a great deal of publicity, but they do make things happen. It is my pleasure to regularly speak at the Peter Lowe seminars conducted around America. The speakers include some of the outstanding business, media, and political leaders of our time. Attendance is enormous and people obviously benefit, because each year the attendance is larger than the previous year. The speakers get all the publicity, but the people who make these success seminars happen are the ones who are responsible for such things as taking orders for tickets, ushering people to their seats, answering questions, and giving directions to the rest rooms and telephones. I don't care how brilliant the speakers might be, if details "behind the scenes" don't take place, the seminar will be a dud. It takes teamwork.

If you get a rise out of your boss instead of a raise, you may be doing something wrong.

Those Excuses We Make

You're not finished when you are defeated, you are finished when you quit.

My brother, the late Judge Ziglar, loved to tell the story of the fellow who went next door to borrow his neighbor's lawn mower. The neighbor explained that he could not let him use the lawn mower because all the flights had been canceled from New York to Los Angeles. The borrower asked him what canceled flights from New York to Los Angeles had to do with borrowing his lawn mower. "It doesn't have anything to do with it, but if I don't want to let you use my lawn mower, one excuse is as good as another."

The neighbor was absolutely right. One excuse is as good as another, because an excuse, in most cases, is nothing but a denial or refusal to accept responsibility. My trusty 1828 *Noah Webster Dictionary* says to *excuse* is "to justify" or "to vindicate," "a plea offered in extenuation of a fault or irregular deportment." George Washington Carver said that 99 percent of failures come from people who have a habit of making excuses. Harold Sherman says, "It's mighty soothing to the ego to be able to alibi our failures. I've done it, you've done it, and it has seemed to help temporarily. But the alibis have proved costly in the long run, because they've kept us from facing the truth about ourselves. They have kept us from going to work and correcting our mistakes, eliminating our weaknesses, developing our talents, improving our character." And finally, "Don't make excuses, make good."

These little gems are invaluable and should force each of us to think. When we do that, we won't make excuses—we will make good.

~

There are about 200,000 useless words in the English language—and many politicians repeatedly use most of them.

The Gratitude Attitude

What you bestow on another has a way of belonging to you forever.

My friend Bill Schiebler is a man who lives by our philosophy that you can have everything in life you want if you will just help enough other people get what they want. Even though Bill has multiple sclerosis, his attitude of gratitude was very apparent as he shared the following incident with me.

Bill explained that his MS causes him to tire easily and one day he was especially exhausted as he drove, very slowly, into his driveway. He knew he really needed to rest and wanted to be "left alone." However, at that particular moment, his electrician (who has two gardens on Bill's land) came briskly walking up and eagerly told Bill that he had planted some vegetables for him. Bill said he thanked him and went inside to take a nap. Sleep eluded him and he wasn't getting "much of a rest." He abruptly sat up in bed, realizing he hadn't acknowledged the electrician's kindness with a very grateful spirit. He got up immediately, went outside to his garden, apologized for his lack of gratitude, and "warmly thanked him the way I should have in the first place."

Bill continued with his story: "The electrician knows I have M.S. He also knows how critical it is that I get my rest. When he realized I had interrupted my nap just to show appreciation for his kind gesture, he beamed at my specific token of gratitude. Know what else? I went back inside and took a restful nap. The electrician went back to his gardening and planted more vegetables for me." As Bill put it, "We both won with that encounter."

Bill concludes: "Feeling gratitude but not specifically expressing it is like wrapping a present but not giving it."

～

Things change. Years ago the principal would have expelled a kid who wore blue jeans, an earring, and a beard. Today, that is the principal. (JOE HICKMAN, CONTEMPORARY COMEDY)

This Mother Is Right

Eyes that look are common; eyes that see are rare.

—J. OSWALD SANDERS

Betty Stephans tells of visiting a friend whose three-year-old daughter frequently interrupted her housework by insisting that her mother "come outside and see." She would then excitedly show her mother a flower, a butterfly, a broken bird's egg, or a crawling ant. After the umpteenth interruption, Betty commented, "You're awfully patient with her, but all these little trips must nearly wreck your daily routine. Don't you ever just want to scream?" "Well," the mother replied cheerfully, "I brought her into the world. The least I can do is let her show it to me."

What a beautiful approach to take! How right and how wise she was. She gave her child a precious gift—her time. The housework will always be there, as any mother will tell you, but the little girl will grow and before you know it, she's out of school, married, and a mother herself.

Studies indicate that virtually all small children have vivid imaginations, but by the time they're ten years old most of their imaginations have been stifled. One of the reasons for that is that parents either do not have, or do not take, the time to share the wonders that children see every day. Parents often fail to see that the stick-horse really is "Trigger in full color," or that the lines on the ground are a spaceship ready to take off. Too bad, because it's of such as this that the little ones grow, develop their imaginations, and become the problem solvers of the future. Think about it. Spend that time with your child. Let the housework sit a while. Otherwise, the little one might not.

≈

For some reason I didn't like that Disney movie. Aladdin *rubbed me the wrong way.* (GARY APPLE)

Do Something Nice Today

You cannot live a perfect day without doing something for someone who will never be able to repay you.

—JOHN WOODEN

America is getting older. Social Security faces a crisis. Many people are wondering what they can do when their work life ends. Neva Marie Mabbott offers some heartwarming thoughts:

"When surgery loomed on my personal horizon, one of my concerns was financial. As a widow living on Social Security and with what I made working three hours a day in a Montessori playground and nap room, I could ill afford to take a month off for recuperation. Fortunately, that worry was nipped in the bud by a call from another widow from my church. 'Neva? This is Madeleine. I just called your boss and made arrangements to keep you on the payroll in December while I work in your place.' 'But I can't let you do that,' I said. But Madaleine replied, 'Now, now, it's all arranged. I've done this kind of work in my home and I'll come in a couple of days before you go to the hospital to learn your routine. Besides, I want you to rest, not worry about a loss of income.'

"My thanks barely made it past the large lump in my throat. December brought rest, reading, and writing time. It was the most beautiful Advent and Christmas of my life. Madeleine is surely a wonderful example of a sacrificial giver."

There's nothing that will make you feel better than doing something for someone else. You might not be able to take a month off, but you could baby-sit for a young mother with errands to run but no money for a baby-sitter. You could spend an hour in a nursing home, loving, talking, and listening to those who are there. You could deliver a few "Meals on Wheels," or help at the Salvation Army as they serve the underprivileged.

∿

A perfect example of the power of prayer is when a blizzard closes the schools on the day of a big exam. (DOUG LARSON)

Legislating Morality

Your values should not be determined by the type of business you have. Rather, your values should govern your business.

—DON MARTIN

Every time issues such as gambling, pornography, prostitution, sleazy television programming, etc., are discussed, there are those who say we cannot "legislate morality." The reality is we can, we have, and we must. It's immoral to kill, and therefore we have laws against murder. It's immoral to steal and we have laws against thievery. It's immoral to abuse someone, so we have laws against assault. We constantly legislate morality; however, the legislation would be more effective if we conscientiously taught morality through the process of teaching values. You don't teach ethics—you teach integrity, because a person of integrity will do things in an ethical manner, provided he knows what the ethical manner is and that's why teaching it is critical.

According to the February 1996 issue of *American Management Association,* some experts argue that ethics and values are learned as a natural part of human development, derived from home, school, religion, and other influences. However, they say that some authorities maintain that ethics, as the innate notion of right and wrong, cannot be taught to an adult. They're saying that an individual has been shaped as honest and upstanding or devious and venal long before he or she sets foot in the business world.

Certainly part of that is true. Some experts maintain that 80 percent of a child's character is formed by the age of five, but to say that ethics and values cannot be taught to adults is erroneous. People can and do change because, basically, all of us will act in our best self-interest if we clearly understand what that best interest is. Evidence is solid that the "good guys," over the long haul, are the big winners in their personal, family, business, and financial lives.

~

The chief ingredient of fad diets is baloney. (DR. NEIL STONE)

Character Makes the Difference

More people fail because of flaws in their character than for any other reason.

—DR. D. JAMES KENNEDY

One philosopher made the observation that if the immoral but knew the value of honesty, thieves and knaves, for their own self-interests, would become honest men. You can check the record books and you will discover that all great failures are character failures and the long-term success stories are people who built their careers on character. Most experts believe that companies have the opportunity, power, and responsibility to teach appropriate behavior to their people.

When character is taught in the corporate culture the benefits extend into the family as well. Our own company has experienced this as we have persuaded the companies we train to permit the families—husbands and wives—of the employees to come in and participate in the training. Results have been outstanding because it gets all the family members on the "same page."

Kate Nelson, senior fellow in ethics at the Wharton School of the University of Pennsylvania, says that there are three kinds of employees in any industry. Those she calls "good soldiers" know the rules and have a good moral compass; "loose cannons" have a good moral compass but don't know the rules. They are full of good intentions but don't read policy manuals. "Grenades" have their own agenda and their activities can blow up and devastate an organization. She points out that even "good soldiers" need steady coaching—and I like the word *steady,* to which I would add "consistent." When we teach the entire company these basic concepts, we will have converted a group of wide-ranging abilities and backgrounds into a team that will produce good results.

~

If someone offers you the world on a silver platter, take the platter. (WALL STREET JOURNAL)

Healthy Fear

Fear God and you need not be afraid of anyone else.
—WOODROW WILSON

There really is "healthy fear." For example, it's very healthy to fear drinking before you drive. However, fear should not be allowed to run rampant through our lives so that it becomes such a devastating factor that it produces failure. The problem is not getting rid of fear, but using it properly. Dr. Judge M. Lyle said, "Someone has said that the basis of action should be love and not fear. Theoretically that is true, but in practice it does not work out that way. There are legitimate fears. Fear of ignorance causes you to seek an education and fear of poverty makes you work. Fear of disease motivates you to practice healthy and sanitary living. Fear of losing your job will inspire you to show up on time and do the best you know how to do. Fear of failing a class will drive a student to spend extra time in the books. Fear of losing our family inspires us to be faithful to them, work hard for them, and show them love on a daily basis."

All of us should certainly have some healthy fear.

There's real fear in walking across a busy street without going to the corner where the lights are arranged for that purpose. There's legitimate fear in driving your car at excessive speeds under any conditions, but particularly when the visibility is poor or the streets are slippery. We must learn to distinguish those helpful fears from the harmful ones. When you can do that, fear is a friend. Until you learn to do it, however, fear can be an enemy.

~

True terror is to wake up one morning and discover that your high school class is running the country. (KURT VONNEGUT)

About the Author

~

ZIG ZIGLAR is chairman of the Zig Ziglar Corporation, which is committed to helping people more fully utilize their physical, mental, and spiritual resources. Ziglar is one of the most sought-after inspirational speakers in the country. He travels around the world delivering his message of hope, humor, and enthusiasm to audiences of all kinds and sizes.

Ziglar is the best-selling author of many books, including *Confessions of a Grieving Christian, Confessions of a Happy Christian, Something to Smile About, Over the Top,* and *See You at the Top,* which has sold more than 1.5 million copies worldwide. He and his wife, Jean, make their home in Dallas, Texas.

More Best-Selling Books
by Zig Ziglar

Confessions of a Grieving Christian

In this uplifting book, Zig Ziglar uses the experience of losing his oldest daughter, Suzan, to encourage you to deal with the reality of loss and learn to take up the threads of life again as you find consolation and inspiration in the Giver of All Peace.

0-8407-9182-8 • Hardcover • 288 pages

Over the Top—Revised and Updated

This sequel to the best-seller *See You at the Top* has been revised and updated with pages full of on-target advice for maximum success and happiness. Ziglar identifies and shows precisely how to achieve what everyone desires most in life—to be happy, healthy, reasonably prosperous, and secure and to have friends, peace of mind, good family relationships, and hope.

0-7852-7119-8 • Hardcover • 336 pages

Something to Smile About

The inspiring stories in this book will give you a daily word of encouragement, which Zig Ziglar calls "the fuel of hope." They will also give you something to smile about and, on occasion, even a healthy laugh.

0-8407-9183-6 • Hardcover • 224 pages